The Headway Readers

President and Publisher
M. Blouke Carus

Executive Vice President
Paul Carus

Education Director
Carl Bereiter

Operations Manager
Ruth A. Berke

Editorial Director
Dale E. Howard

**Coordinator of Editorial
Services**
Juanita A. Raman

Production Manager
LeRoy Ceresa

Art Director
Todd Sanders

Project Leader
Marilyn F. Cunningham

Associate Editor
Catherine E. Anderson

Assistant Editor
Diane M. Sikora

From Sea to Sea

The Headway Program
Level E

Editor
Marianne Carus

Reading and Language Arts Curriculum Development Center
André W. Carus, Director

Open Court   La Salle, Illinois

ACKNOWLEDGMENTS:

FOR PERMISSION to reprint copyrighted material, grateful acknowledgment is made to the following publishers and persons:

Coward-McCann, Inc., and Russell & Volkening, Inc., for *George Washington's Breakfast*, text copyright © 1969 by Jean Fritz, reprinted by permission.

Harper & Row, Publishers, and Methuen & Co., Ltd. for "The Story of Grandpa's Sled and the Pig," and illustrations, from *Little House in the Big Woods* by Laura Ingalls Wilder, illustrated by Garth Williams, copyright 1932, as to text, and 1953, as to pictures.

Hart Publishing Company for "Johnny Appleseed" from *A Treasury of the World's Great Myths and Legends* by Joanna Strong and Tom B. Leonard, copyright 1951 by the Hart Publishing Company.

Holt, Rinehart and Winston, Inc. for "Backward Rhyme," "The Horse and the Flea," and "Way Down South" from *A Rocket in My Pocket,* compiled by Carl Withers, copyright 1948 by Carl Withers.

Houghton Mifflin Company for "My First Buffalo Hunt" from *My Indian Boyhood* by Chief Standing Bear, copyright 1931 by Houghton Mifflin Company.

Little, Brown and Co. for "Patrick O'Donnell and the Leprechaun" from *Favorite Fairy Tales Told in Ireland* retold by Virginia Haviland, text copyright © 1961 by Virginia Haviland.

Rand McNally & Company for "Pioneers Go West in Covered Wagons" from *Our Country's Story* by Frances Cavanah, copyright 1945 by Rand McNally & Company, publishers.

All possible care has been taken to trace ownership and obtain permission for each selection included. If any errors or omissions have occurred, they will be corrected in subsequent editions, provided they are brought to the publisher's attention.

Contents

Part One: Our Country Long Ago

Part Two: Stories and Poems Everyone Likes

Part Three: Famous Americans

Part Four: Our Country Today

Part Five: For Readers Brave and Bold

Part Six: On Your Own

ILLUSTRATORS:
Ray App (110), George Armstrong (59, 83, 136, 137), Melanie Arwin (65, 86, 89, 91), Cary (37, 47, 57, 66, 70), Joseph Cellini (16, 50-52, 54, 113, 115, 117, 131, 138, 140, 148, 153), David Cunningham (5, 7), Mike Eagle (123), Robert Frankenberg (156), Imero Gobatto (63), Robin Jacques (25), Faith Jaques (78, 81), Victor Mays (13, 15, 18, 19, 21, 29, 33, 34, 35, 45, 105, 120, 145, 158), Charles McBarron (10, 40, 101), National Aeronautics and Space Administration (3), Dan Siculan (166, 170, 177, 181), Sally Springer (74, 76), Richard Stalzer (164, 184), Al Stine (22, 23), Jozef Sumichrast (cover), Benjamin West (102, 111), Garth Williams (92, 96).

PHOTOGRAPHY:
Julian Caraballo/Tom Stack & Associates (129), Robert Frerck/Odyssey Productions (23), The General Electric Company & NASA (3).

DESIGN:
John Grandits, James Buddenbaum.

Part One

Our Country
Long Ago

OUR COUNTRY

How does our country look to an astronaut high above the earth? What would you see of our country if you were flying around the earth so high in the sky?

An astronaut sees the big things first. There is so much more water than land that you would see the great oceans around our country. You will see that our country is just a part of a big piece of land that we call North America. Way up north you will see Alaska and Canada. South of our country you will see Mexico.

Looking down at our country, you might then want to find the places that mean most to you. You would see rivers and the Great Lakes and the mountains in the East and West. You would look for the places that you knew when you were on earth. You would be thinking of your family and friends and your home. You would be so far, far above our country that our land would be spread out like a map below you. To you our country would look like the picture on the opposite page. Compare the picture with the maps on pages 164 and 184 of this book.

WORDS TO WATCH		
astronaut	Canada	explorers
North America	Mexico	pioneers
Alaska	Great Lakes	United States
earth	opposite	country

Understanding maps of your own block, your street, your path to school, your city, and your state will help you understand any map of our country.

This book will tell you how our country grew to be the way it is. It will tell you about our early explorers, our brave pioneers, and our great men and women.

When you have read this book from cover to cover, you will understand better why our country is a great country, and you will be very glad that you live in it.

QUESTIONS

1. Look at the map of the United States on page 184, and tell the names of the oceans which touch our country. What are the names of the countries which touch our country? What else can you learn from a map?

2. What are the names of the mountain ranges in the United States? The lakes? The rivers?

3. Look at the maps of our country on pages 164 and 184 of your book. What can you learn from them?

4. What states have you visited? What big cities? What important places?

5. What do you think can be done to make our country a better country?

How America Was Discovered

One sunny day in Italy, a long time ago, a boy named Christopher Columbus was sitting on the seashore looking out over the water.

"I'm going to be a sailor when I grow up," he said to himself. "I want to sail the seas to faraway lands."

WORDS TO WATCH

Italy	monsters	*Pinta*
Christopher Columbus	sea serpents	*Niña*
ocean	voyage	island
India	Atlantic Ocean	nightingale
Isabella	*Santa María*	generous
Spain	Indies	America

Columbus loved the ocean, and when he grew up he did become a great sailor.

In Columbus's time, people did not know much about the world—many of them thought it was flat. But Columbus thought it was round. He said that he could sail around the world just as a fly can walk around an apple.

Columbus wanted most of all to go to India because India was a rich country. In those days people went to India by traveling east, but because Columbus thought the world was round, he wanted to reach India by sailing west.

Columbus was a poor man. He had no ships and no money. When he asked people to help him, most of them only laughed at him and thought he was out of his mind. But he kept on trying, and he did gain some important friends.

Finally he went to Isabella, the queen of Spain. After a few years, the queen gave Columbus three ships and wished him good luck. But Columbus still needed a crew of sailors.

Sailors did not want to go on the voyage because they were afraid that they would never see their homes again. They had heard stories about monsters and sea serpents attacking ships and killing the sailors. Finally Columbus was able to gather a crew of 88 men.

At last the ships were ready. Columbus and his sailors set out across the Atlantic Ocean in the *Santa María,* the *Pinta,* and the *Niña.* The ships sailed for many days, and the farther the ships went, the more frightened the sailors became.

At last they said to Columbus, "We have been on the ocean for more than thirty days, and still there is no sight of land. We are hungry and afraid. We will go no farther."

But Columbus answered, "Wait a few more days. If by that time we have not found land, we will turn around and go back." The very next day the sailors saw a bird, and then they knew that land must be near. The following morning, October 12, 1492, they heard the cry "Land ho!" There ahead of them lay a beautiful island. The sailors cheered and sang songs and the ships' cannons boomed. When the sailors reached shore, they kissed the ground because they were so glad to be on land again. They begged Columbus's pardon for wanting to give up the voyage and return home.

On the way home from his first trip across the Atlantic Ocean, Columbus wrote about the lands and the Indians he had seen.

"The lands are all most beautiful and full of trees so high

they seem to reach to the sky. The nightingale was singing and, too, other birds of a thousand sorts. The people of this island, and of all the others that I have found and seen, are kind and generous with what they have.

"When I first came to the Indies, they thought I had come from heaven. They ran from house to house and to the nearby villages with loud cries of 'Come! Come to see the people from heaven!'"

Columbus thought that the island he had discovered was near India; he did not know that it lay next to a new continent.

QUESTIONS

1. Where did Columbus want to go with his ships?
2. Who gave him the ships to make the voyage?
3. Why were the sailors afraid to go on the voyage?
4. Why were the sailors glad when they saw a bird?
5. What did Columbus write about his discovery?
6. Do you think Columbus was a brave man? Why?

Pocahontas and Captain John Smith

When Columbus returned to Spain, he brought back all sorts of things from America that people had never seen before. He brought back pieces of cotton, strange-looking wood carvings, and even stranger-looking birds and animals. He also brought back some Indians, and, to people in Europe, they seemed the strangest of all.

Columbus told many wonderful stories about the land he had discovered. Soon, people from all over Europe wanted to see this new land for themselves. One of them was Captain John Smith. In the year 1607, he and some other men and women came to America from England and built a little town called Jamestown.

The people who built Jamestown did not have much food and many became sick. Captain John Smith became their leader. He learned the Indian language and traded with the Indians to get food.

In one of his books, Captain Smith tells how he killed an Indian of a friendly tribe. He was then captured by other In-

---

WORDS TO WATCH		
Pocahontas	prisoner	punishment
Captain John Smith	warriors	England
language	protect	Europe

dians of that tribe and taken before their chief. The Indian chief said that Captain Smith's punishment should be death.

The Indian chief had a beautiful daughter named Pocahontas. When Pocahontas saw that Captain Smith was taken prisoner by Indian warriors, she felt sorry for him. She could see that he was a brave man.

When she saw that the Indians were going to kill him, she ran up to him. She asked the Indians not to beat him, and she held his head in her arms to protect him.

Finally the Indian chief ordered the Indians not to kill Captain John Smith. Pocahontas had saved his life. Later she became a Christian, married an Englishman, and went to England. She was given many honors.

QUESTIONS
---

1. What did Columbus bring back to Spain?
2. Why was Captain John Smith a good leader?
3. Who was Pocahontas?
4. Why did Pocahontas want to save Captain John Smith?
5. Find out more about Jamestown.

THE INDIANS

The Indians found America long before Columbus did. They came to America so long ago that no one knows exactly where they came from. Many people think they came from Siberia, and walked across to Alaska on a piece of dry land. Others believe they sailed across the Pacific Ocean.

The Indians were the first Americans. Columbus called them Indians because he thought he had landed near India. We still call them Indians because Columbus did, even though America is very far from India.

The Indians taught the settlers many things. Did you know that potatoes and tomatoes and corn were first raised by Indians? They showed the settlers how to grow pumpkins and squash and beans too.

They knew how to start a fire with flint stones. They also knew how to talk to their friends far away by sending different kinds of smoke puffs into the air.

There were Indians in almost every part of North and South America when Columbus landed. The next stories will tell you some interesting facts about the American Indians.

QUESTIONS

1. Why are the American Indians called Indians?
2. What vegetables did the Indians grow?
3. What else did the Indians know?

Spelling Words to Watch

I. Read and Spell

half	nature	cousin
ache	buy	straight
guess	answer	minute
niece	once	station
cough	through	sure
built	fruit	friend
suit	their	busy
enough	chorus	piece
special	whistle	gnat
sugar	often	believe

II. Read and Answer

1. Why do you think each of these words is hard to spell?
2. Which of these words do you think is the hardest to spell?
3. Think of some other words that are hard to spell.

III. Write

1. Write five sentences, each one using two of the words in the lists on this page.
2. Write three sentences, each one using three of the words in the lists on this page.

The Indians of the East

The Indians who lived in the eastern part of the United States were hunters and farmers. They tracked animals silently in the thick forests, they fished in the swift streams, and they grew many crops.

An Indian hunter had to bring home fresh deer meat, or his family would be disappointed. He had to find deer tracks and follow them quietly until he could see the deer. He could not step on a dry twig, or the deer would hear him and dash away into the forest.

When he was close to the deer, he would draw an arrow

WORDS TO WATCH

streams	tobacco	wigwams
disappointed	kernels	canoes
quiver		

from his quiver and place it in his bow. He would aim the arrow and—Z-I-N-G—he would shoot to kill!

The Indian men did the hunting, and the Indian women did the farming. They grew corn, tobacco, beans, and squash. They pounded the kernels of corn into meal and boiled it in water to make corn meal mush. Sometimes they put maple sugar in the corn meal to make it sweet.

Some Indians in the eastern part of the United States lived in wigwams. Wigwams were big enough for only one family. Others lived in longhouses, which looked like long barns made of logs and bark from trees. Several families lived together in one longhouse.

The roads of that time were the many lakes and rivers in the eastern part of the United States. The Indians traveled along these lakes and rivers in canoes. They made their canoes from the bark of elm trees or birch trees. The Indians could travel quickly over the water in these light canoes or carry them over land to the next river or lake.

The Indians of the East knew how to use all the good things that nature gave them.

1. How did the Indians of the East get their food?
2. What did the Indian women do?
3. How did the Indians of the East travel?
4. What did the Indians of the East live in?

BACKWARD RHYME

American Folk Rhyme

One bright day in the middle of the night,
Two dead boys got up to fight.
Back to back they faced each other,
Drew their swords and shot each other.
A deaf policeman heard the noise,
Came and shot the two dead boys.
If you do not believe this lie is true,
Ask the blind man; he saw it too.

The Plains Indians

The Great Plains in the middle of the United States are miles of open rolling country without many trees. The Indians who lived there were called the Plains Indians.

Long ago thousands and thousands of buffalo roamed the Great Plains. The Plains Indians killed these buffalo for food, for clothing, for shelter, and for almost everything else they needed.

WORDS TO WATCH

Great Plains	tepees	papoose
buffalo	Spanish	deerskin
roamed	tanned	buckskin
herds	moccasins	cradleboard

From time to time the Plains Indians had to move their camps to follow the buffalo herds. The whole tribe gathered up their belongings, including their tepees.

At first these Indians did not have horses, but when the Spanish came to America, they brought horses with them. Some of these horses went wild, and the Indians learned to tame and ride them.

The Indians became very good at hunting buffalo from galloping horses. Sometimes they ran the buffalo over a steep cliff and killed a thousand buffalo at one time. By slicing and drying the buffalo meat, the Indians could save most of the meat to eat later.

The women of the Plains Indian tribes did not grow corn as the Indian women of the eastern tribes did. Instead they

tanned buffalo skins and made clothing. They removed the hair from the skin of the buffalo and washed the skins in a nearby river. They rubbed oil into the skins and finally smoked them. In this way the buffalo skins could be used to make tepees.

The women made clothes from deerskin or buckskin. They used beads to decorate clothes and belts and moccasins.

An Indian mother liked to carry her papoose with her wherever she went. She wrapped her baby in a buckskin blanket and then strapped it to a cradleboard. She tied the cradleboard to her back and always knew her papoose was close by.

QUESTIONS

1. Find the Great Plains on the map on page 164 of your book.
2. How did the Plains Indians kill buffalo?
3. What did the Indians use buffalo for?
4. How did the Plains Indian women spend their time?
5. Why did the Plains Indians move around so much?
6. How were the Plains Indians different from the Indians who lived in the East?

The Indians of the Northwest

The Indians of the northwest coast of America knew how to hunt whales and seals and how to catch salmon.

Hunting whales was very dangerous because the Indians had only war canoes, which are much smaller than whales. When the canoe got close to the whale, the leader threw his harpoon at the whale, and then the other Indians in the canoe did the same. One end of a rope was tied to a harpoon, and the other end was tied to the boat.

The whale is a huge animal. It usually swims for a long

WORDS TO WATCH

northwest coast	salmon	lodges
seal	harpoon	totem pole

time before it dies. A wounded whale could pull a canoe far out into the ocean.

The Indians of the Northwest caught salmon with spears or in traps. Indian boys knew how to spear salmon. An Indian boy would stand on the bank of a river at the foot of a waterfall and wait for the salmon to swim up near the falls. Then he would aim his spear at a big salmon and throw it.

The Indians of the Northwest did not have to move around as much as the Plains Indians did, so they built strong houses called lodges. These were made of big cedar trees, cut down with stone hatchets. Lodges were big enough for many families to live in.

Outside the lodge, the Indians would put up a totem pole. These totem poles were very tall, with faces and animals carved on them, one on top of another. Some of these faces looked very strange and frightening. Totem poles told a story, and the Indians of each tribe knew what these stories were. But totem poles do not talk, and from us they keep their stories a secret.

Other Indians

Not all American Indians were hunters or food gatherers. In the valleys of the Mississippi and Ohio rivers lived the Mound Builders. They take that name from the burial mounds they built. Some of their mounds were eighty feet high.

The Mound Builders lived in log huts. Their towns were surrounded by walls made of stakes. They grew corn, squash, and pumpkins. They spun fibers of nettles, grass, fur, and hair, and wove cloth. They made beautiful bracelets, breastplates, and helmets out of copper, mica, beaten silver, and pearls. They traded in distant places. They formed a great nation stretching over hundreds of miles.

In the American Southwest the Pueblo Indians—*pueblo* is the Spanish word for town—built their square houses out of stone, wood, and mortar on the top of high mesas. Like an apartment, each house had many rooms. The Pueblos cut timbers from forests many miles away. They irrigated their crops. In one valley, more than a million acres of farmland were irrigated by the Pueblos. Their art and religion have much to teach non-Pueblo people. Young Pueblos today may have had ancestors in America for ten thousand years.

WORDS TO WATCH		
burial	mortar	ancestor
mica	bracelet	mesa
nettle	breastplate	irrigate

QUESTION

How were the Mound Builders and Pueblos different from some other Indians?

The Pilgrims

In the middle of the Atlantic Ocean, a little ship was tossed about in a fierce storm. The lightning cracked, the thunder roared, and huge waves washed over the decks.

"It's a terrible night," said Captain Jones. "I hope we live through it."

"We'll live through it," replied William Brewster. "Nothing will keep us from reaching America. It is God's will."

WORDS TO WATCH

Pilgrims	lightning	William Brewster
Atlantic Ocean	Captain Jones	*Mayflower*

The name of this little ship was the *Mayflower,* and the people on it called themselves Pilgrims. The Pilgrims were English people, but they did not want to live in England any longer because the king would not let them worship God as they wished.

For many weeks the *Mayflower* tossed about on the ocean, but at last it reached America. As soon as the Pilgrims set foot on the land, they thanked God for bringing them safely to their new home.

The Pilgrims landed in America in the middle of winter, so they had to build a shelter at once. At first they built a log house big enough to hold all of them, but later they built houses for each family.

The winter was long and cold. Sometimes they did not have enough to eat, and before spring came, many of them had become sick and died.

The only people the Pilgrims met were Indians. At first the Pilgrims were afraid of the Indians, but the Indian chief was very friendly. He brought other Indians to talk with the Pilgrims, and soon the Indians and the Pilgrims were good friends.

In the spring the *Mayflower* went back to England. The Pilgrims watched longingly as the ship sailed away without them, but they had made their choice. It was right for them to stay. This was their new land, their home, and now they were free to worship as they pleased.

1. Why did the Pilgrims leave England?
2. Why was life hard for the Pilgrims in America?
3. How did the Indians act toward the Pilgrims?
4. When the *Mayflower* went back to England, why did the Pilgrims not go back to England too?
5. Find out more about the Pilgrims.
6. What is Plymouth Rock, and where is it?
7. Find Plymouth on the map of the United States on page 184 of your book.

The North Wind Doth Blow

Anonymous

The north wind doth blow,
And we shall have snow,
And what will poor robin do then?
  Poor thing!

He'll sit in a barn,
And to keep himself warm,
Will hide his head under his wing.
  Poor thing!

The First Thanksgiving

During the first winter in America, the Pilgrims suffered terribly. They had only a few small huts, and many died of sickness and hunger.

In the springtime, the Pilgrims and the Indians became friends.

An Indian named Squanto showed them how to plant corn —four kernels to each hillock. He also showed them how to catch herring from the brook to use for food. Then he showed them how to tap maple trees for their sugary sap and where to find fat eels.

That first summer, life was no longer so cruel. The Pilgrims' crops ripened in the sun. The first autumn was beautiful, and the harvest was rich. The Pilgrims were thankful to be alive, so they planned a day of Thanksgiving for a harvest feast.

Squanto was sent to invite the braves to the feast. Four Pilgrims went hunting and returned with enough ducks and

WORDS TO WATCH		
Squanto	eels	venison
kernels	braves	lobster
hillock	Plymouth	costumes
herring	upset	feathers
brook	ornaments	Thanksgiving

28

geese for a week. They shot wild turkeys too, for there were many of them near Plymouth.

When the Indians arrived, ninety strong, they saw that the Pilgrims were upset. They could not feed so many. The chief understood and sent a few men to the forest. They returned, bringing five deer to share. Then the Indians and Pilgrims sat down to eat goose and venison, lobster, eel pie, corn, bread, salad, plums, berries, and red and white wine. The Indians had such a good time that they stayed for three days. They dressed up in their best costumes with bright feathers and gay ornaments to dance and sing.

Finally the first Thanksgiving came to an end, and the Indians went back through the forest to their homes.

Every year, after the harvest in late November, we still set aside a day of Thanksgiving to remind us of the Pilgrims and to give thanks for all the good things that are in our country.

1. Why did the Pilgrims have a Thanksgiving Day?
2. What did they eat on the first Thanksgiving?
3. What did the Indians bring to the feast?
4. What happened after the feast?
5. Why do we still have a Thanksgiving Day every year?

good tidings
Anonymous

A sunshiny shower
Won't last half an hour.

Rain before seven
Stops before eleven.

March winds and April showers
Bring forth beautiful May flowers.

Verbs to Watch

I. Read and Spell

Today I	Yesterday I	Many times I have
see	saw	seen
go	went	gone
do	did	done
eat	ate	eaten
drink	drank	drunk
begin	began	begun
fall	fell	fallen
know	knew	known

II. Read and Answer

1. What are the other two forms of these verbs?

   grow   bite   speak   swim   take   ring
   sing   drive   sit   swing   throw   fly

2. Can you think of some other tricky verbs?

III. Write

Write five sentences using some of the verbs listed above. Be sure to use verbs from all three lists in Part I.

Early Explorers of Our Country

The English explored and settled the eastern part of our country. But the Spanish had earlier claimed land in the south, and the French came down from the north.

A hundred years before the Pilgrims came ashore at Plymouth, the Spanish began to conquer the lands below what is now Texas. Some of the names of the Spanish explorers were Cortés, Coronado, and Ponce de León.

Often they were cruel to the Indians, whose gold they wanted. The Spanish leaders were very stubborn. Cortés burned his ships when he landed, so that his men could not leave if they lost their courage. They had to advance, for there was no way for them to retreat.

Not all the Spaniards were cruel. Some, like a priest named Serra, spent their lives teaching and helping the Indians. Serra founded many churches on the West Coast of our country.

WORDS TO WATCH

English	Ponce de León	Canadian settlement
Spanish	priest	Iowa
French	Serra	Illinois tribe
Texas	Florida	mush
Cortés	California	Canada
Coronado	Marquette	Joliet

From Florida to California, the Spanish brought their language and way of life. "Florida" means "full of flowers" in Spanish. "California" is the name of a treasure island in a Spanish story.

The first white men to see the American Midwest were Frenchmen who came from Canadian settlements. About fifty years after the Pilgrims sat down to their Thanksgiving feast, Marquette and Joliet took birch canoes down the Wisconsin River to the Mississippi River. They were sent as missionaries to preach to the Indians and as traders to buy furs from them. Marquette was a priest and Joliet a trader.

For two weeks the travelers paddled down the river, and in all this time they did not see a single Indian. After they had gone hundreds of miles in this way, they came to a place where they saw tracks in the mud. This part of the country is now called the state of Iowa.

Marquette and Joliet left their friends in the canoes and followed the tracks. After walking two hours, they came to an Indian village. They sneaked up near enough to hear the Indians talking, but the Indians did not see them.

Joliet and Marquette did not know whether the Indians would kill them or not, so they said a short prayer. Then they stood out in full view and gave a loud shout.

The Indians swarmed out of their homes like bees and stared at the strangers. Then four Indians came toward them carrying a peace pipe, which they held up toward the sun. This meant that they were friendly.

These were Indians of the Illinois tribe, and they took Joliet and Marquette into their village. As they came to a large wigwam, they met a chief who stood in the doorway.

He said, "Frenchmen, how bright the sun shines when you come to see us! We are all waiting for you. You shall now come into our houses in peace."

The Illinois Indians made a feast for their new friends. First they had mush of corn meal with fat meat in it. One of the Indians fed the Frenchmen as if they were babies by putting the mush into their mouths with a large spoon.

This same Indian then put pieces of fish into the visitors' mouths after he had picked out the bones with his fingers. The roast dog that followed was not so tasty, but the Frenchmen liked the buffalo meat.

The next morning 600 of the Illinois Indians went with the Frenchmen to the Mississippi River to say good-bye. The Indians gave the Frenchmen a peace pipe to carry with them and wished them a safe journey back to Canada.

QUESTIONS
---

1. Besides the English, who were the other main explorers?
2. Why did Cortés burn his ships?
3. What did Marquette and Joliet set out to do?
4. Follow the route of Marquette and Joliet on the map on page 164. Find where Texas, Florida, and California are.
5. What things did the Illinois Indians do to show that they were friendly to Marquette and Joliet?

OUR COUNTRY'S BIRTHDAY

Our country's birthday is the Fourth of July, which is one of our great holidays. We celebrate the Fourth of July because we want to remember the day our country was born. On that day there are parades and picnics, and when night comes, many people gather to watch fireworks light up the sky.

At first our country was only a group of colonies. There were thirteen American colonies, and they all belonged to England. But England is a country far across the Atlantic Ocean, and the king of England did not care much about the people who lived in America. He tried to make them obey laws and pay taxes that they thought were unfair.

The leaders of the American colonies wanted America to be free from England. One of these leaders was Thomas Jefferson. He wrote the Declaration of Independence, which told the world that America was going to make itself free from England.

For seventeen days Jefferson sat at his desk and wrote and rewrote. He had always believed that people could rule

---

WORDS TO WATCH

free	taxes	Declaration of Independence
right	created	Thomas Jefferson
colonies	equal	Atlantic Ocean
fireworks	holidays	England

themselves, and so he thought that they should be free. He was not a soldier like George Washington, but he fought for what he believed was right. He fought with his pen.

His words in the Declaration of Independence have become famous around the world. Men are still fighting for the freedom he wrote about.

In the Declaration of Independence, Jefferson wrote, "All men are created equal." He also said that the poor and the rich have the same right to live and be free and happy.

On the Fourth of July in the year 1776, the leaders of the American colonies voted for the Declaration of Independence. On this day our country was born. A few days later the leaders told the people what they had done. When the people heard the good news, they shouted, "Hooray for the United States." The thirteen colonies became the first thirteen states of the United States of America.

The people never forgot our nation's birthday, and we continue to celebrate it still.

QUESTIONS
---

1. How do people celebrate the Fourth of July?
2. Why did the American people want to be free from England?
3. When was America's birthday?
4. What is the Declaration of Independence?
5. What did Jefferson write in the Declaration of Independence?

States of the United States

I. Read and Pronounce

Alabama	Louisiana	North Dakota
Alaska	Maine	Ohio
Arizona	Maryland	Oklahoma
Arkansas	Massachusetts	Oregon
California	Michigan	Pennsylvania
Colorado	Minnesota	Rhode Island
Connecticut	Mississippi	South Carolina
Delaware	Missouri	South Dakota
Florida	Montana	Tennessee
Georgia	Nebraska	Texas
Hawaii	Nevada	Utah
Idaho	New Hampshire	Vermont
Illinois	New Jersey	Virginia
Indiana	New Mexico	Washington
Iowa	New York	West Virginia
Kansas	North Carolina	Wisconsin
Kentucky		Wyoming

II. Read and Answer

1. Find the states on the map on page 184.
2. Find out which states touch your state.

III. Write

Write about the state you live in or the state you like best.

39

How Our Country Became Free

The Declaration of Independence was signed and all thirteen American colonies demanded to be free from English rule. But the king of England said that the colonies still belonged to England, so he sent soldiers to fight the Americans.

The Americans had many difficulties while fighting the British. They had no trained army, few guns and cannons, and no navy. People thought the Americans could not win the war for freedom.

But many Americans wanted to be free more than anything else. They asked George Washington to lead their army because they knew he was a brave soldier and a great leader. Under his direction the American colonists fought against the British soldiers. This war was called the Revolutionary War.

One of the most important battles of the war was fought at Saratoga. General Gates was the leader of the American soldiers there. One day a scout came into the headquarters of General Gates.

"What news do you bring?" General Gates asked.

"The British are only four miles away, and they are moving toward the camp," the scout replied.

Then the Americans knew that this battle could decide the whole war. If they lost, New England would be cut off from the other colonies. Many volunteers streamed in to help the American army.

The next day the British army was at Saratoga, and the battle was on! Gates attacked first and forced the British back. The British fought hard, but the American sharpshooters pushed back one line and then another. General Arnold, second in command, smashed into the English lines, and there was much hand-to-hand fighting. Just as evening came, General Arnold was wounded. But he shouted, "Carry on! Carry on! Victory is ours!"

Then the unbelievable happened. The Americans surrounded the British, and a few days later the British surrendered.

The Battle of Saratoga showed other countries that the Americans could win important battles. Soon afterward France agreed to help the Americans and sent over ships with men and supplies.

After seven hard years of fighting, the Americans won the war. The British had to give up their thirteen colonies. The colonies became the United States of America.

The Americans had to fight hard to earn their freedom. Today we remember the many brave soldiers who gave their lives so that our country could be free.

WORDS TO WATCH

Revolutionary War	rule	cannon
George Washington	headquarters	British
General Arnold	General Gates	unbelievable
sharpshooters	New England	freedom
Saratoga	volunteers	

QUESTIONS

1. Why did the Americans fight a war against England?
2. What is this war called?
3. Where was an important battle fought?
4. Why did the Americans almost lose the war?
5. Who helped the Americans win the war?

LEWIS AND CLARK

When Thomas Jefferson was president, he wanted to learn more about the western part of America. He sent Lewis and Clark to find out as much as they could about the animals, the mountains, and the Indians of the Great West.

Lewis and Clark needed someone with them who could speak with the Indians to the north and west, especially the Pahkees and the Shoshones. They chose a man who was part Indian and part French. His Indian wife, Sacajawea, came too. She was a Shoshone who had lived among the Pahkees. Her name means "Bird Woman."

Lewis and Clark were afraid at first that a woman would be in the way on such a trip. But later they found that many tribes greeted them with friendliness when they saw Sacajawea. She was a sign to the Indians that the explorers came in peace.

With her papoose strapped to her back, Sacajawea and her husband became guides for Lewis and Clark. They went through many dangers and difficulties with the two great ex-

WORDS TO WATCH		
Thomas Jefferson	wilderness	guides
Lewis	Sacajawea	explorers
Clark	papoose	Shoshones
Great West	Pacific Ocean	St. Louis
	Pahkees	

plorers. Once they almost starved. Another time, Clark and Sacajawea were caught in a great storm. The place where they were standing for shelter began to fill up with water. They were helped out of that dangerous place by York.

York was the first black man the Indians had ever seen. He stood over six feet tall. He was strong, kind, and dignified. But he also liked to join with the other men in making the Indians laugh. York helped to build canoes. He hunted for buffalo, bear, and antelope. One night a buffalo charged through the camp. It almost trampled Clark. The next morning, York found that his rifle had been bent by the buffalo's feet.

The explorers had many narrow escapes from grizzly bears, too. One day six men went hunting. All six of them shot a huge bear, but the bear kept charging at them. Two men jumped into the river to save their lives, but the bear jumped right in after them. Finally, one man on the river bank shot the bear through the head and killed it.

The explorers ate whatever animals they could kill. But it was hard to make good meals in the wilderness. Sacajawea knew where to find "wapato," or wild potato. She would dig them up and put them in soups. She knew how to break and boil elk bones to get the most out of them. She could mend clothes with her needles of small bird bones and thread of hide. She also made leather moccasins for the explorers.

She led the explorers to the place where her own tribe lived. As they got closer, the explorers divided into two groups.

Lewis went by land, Clark by river. Sacajawea was with Clark.

Lewis was the first to see a Shoshone. The Indian brave was riding a horse. As Lewis came near, the Indian turned and rode away. Lewis was disappointed. He needed to trade with the Shoshones for horses to cross the mountains.

Later that day, he met three Indian women. They said they would lead him to the Shoshone camp. As they were on their way, sixty Indians on horseback rode toward them. They were Shoshones. When they saw Lewis and his party, the Shoshones greeted them in peace. They held a feast and danced till midnight.

But the Shoshones feared that their enemies, the Pahkees, might be using Lewis to trap them. Lewis tried to calm them. He gave the chief his gun and told him to use it as he thought best. He dressed like a Shoshone to show that he did not fear a Pahkee attack.

Finally, Clark arrived. When Sacajawea saw the members

of her own tribe, she began to dance for joy. The Shoshones also laughed and sang.

That evening, Lewis and Clark sat down with the Indians and traded for the horses they needed.

It took two years and four months for Lewis and Clark to travel to the Pacific Ocean and back. Many thought they would never return alive. But when they came back to St. Louis, everyone who could walk came to the celebration.

QUESTIONS

1. What did President Jefferson tell Lewis and Clark to do?
2. How did York and Sacajawea help Lewis and Clark?
3. What do you think were some of the dangers these men faced?
4. Why was it important for Lewis and Clark to make this trip?

Raindrops

Softly the rain goes pitter-patter,
Softly the rain comes falling down.
Hark to the people who hurry by;
Raindrops are footsteps from out of the sky!
Softly the rain goes pitter-patter,
Softly the rain comes falling down.

Pioneers Go West
in Covered Wagons

Frances Cavanah

More and more pioneers went west to live. Some of them went to Texas, others to Oregon. Anyone willing to work hard could own a farm out west.

When gold was found in California, people all over the world were excited.

"Let's go to California and get rich," they said. "The gold is in the ground. All we have to do is dig it up."

WORDS TO WATCH		
Texas	covered wagon	keeping watch
Oregon	banjo	guard
California	circle	figures

Most of the pioneers rode west in big covered wagons or on horseback. Several families went together so that they could help one another. At night the wagons were drawn up in a circle. Campfires were lighted, and the women cooked supper. Afterward someone played a banjo while the others sang:

"O California! That's the land for me,
I'm going to California, the gold dust for to see."

When bedtime came, the people and animals slept inside the circle of wagons. The men took turns keeping watch.

West of the Mississippi they traveled across plains and mountains. This was a wild land where only Indians lived. The Indians did not want the white people to come into their country. They attacked the wagons whenever they had a chance.

Often the guard saw dark figures creeping along the ground. "Indians!" he shouted. "The Indians are coming."

The pioneers grabbed their guns. Shot after shot rang out until the Indians were driven off their hunting grounds. Many Indians and also many white people were killed in these attacks. Other pioneers were caught in snowstorms when they crossed the mountains. But they went on and on until they came to California.

Taking their picks and shovels, many of the men began digging in the ground for gold. Some of them became rich.

Others found no gold at all. But they found something much better—a rich, beautiful land of tall trees and fruits and flowers.

Many of the pioneers stayed in California, and they made the beautiful cities and farms and roads that you can see for yourself today.

QUESTIONS

1. Why did the pioneers go to California?
2. What dangers did the pioneers face in traveling westward?
3. What did the pioneers find that was better than gold?
4. Find out more about the California Gold Rush.

Way Down South

American Folk Rhyme

Way down South where bananas grow,
A grasshopper stepped on an elephant's toe.
The elephant said with tears in his eyes,
"Pick on somebody your own size."

The Great Pacific Railroad

Helen Webber

Many people from all over the world wanted to come and live in the American West. But few could stand the hardships and dangers of travel by covered wagon and horseback. Americans began to talk of building a railroad all the way across the country, from the Atlantic to the Pacific.

The first railroads were horse-drawn wagons running on wooden rails. A man would set his wagon on the rails, then hitch up his horse and start off. The wooden rails made a smooth road. Still, this was quite a hard, slow way to travel.

WORDS TO WATCH		
locomotive	Irish	homestead
Civil War	terriers	industrial
Omaha	accent	stampedes
Sacramento		Sierra Nevada

Then all of that was changed by the invention of the steam locomotive—the "Iron Horse." The Iron Horse could make the dream of a great Pacific railroad come true.

It was the time of the Civil War between the Northern and Southern states. The government needed a railroad. But it could not build a railroad and fight a war at the same time. It gave land to two railroad companies. The Union Pacific company was to build westward from Omaha, Nebraska. The Central Pacific company was to build eastward from Sacramento, California, until the two lines met.

To lay the iron rails for the steam locomotive, a level road had to be built. Some people said that a railroad couldn't be built through the desert. Others said that it couldn't be built through the mountains. But the railroad builders blasted and dug through the mountains and deserts and Indian country. They lived through buffalo stampedes and landslides. And they did it all in a shorter time than anyone had thought possible—less than seven years.

The people who built the railroad were mostly newcomers to America. They poured their strength and spirit into their new land. They learned to love it, and they made it their own. Some of the people who came to work on the railroad were Irish, and others were Chinese.

The Irish came to Omaha to work for the Union Pacific. They dug their way across the prairie like terriers digging for bones. "Tarriers" they called themselves, in the accent of their native land. Part of the tarriers' job was fighting off the Indians. The Indians had been pushed farther and farther west by the settlers. They did not want to be driven out again. They did everything they could to stop the Iron Horse from coming in and spoiling their hunting grounds.

At the same time out in the Far West, thousands of Chinese had come to work for the Central Pacific. The task ahead of them was to build the railroad across the Sierra Nevada mountains. This they did, working only with saws and picks and shovels and charges of black powder. Sometimes they worked while hanging over the mountainside in baskets. Sometimes they tunneled through mountains in the dead of winter. Many men died in falls and landslides.

As the two lines came closer and closer together, the Irish and the Chinese began to race to see who could lay the most track. Newspapers reported the race, and people bet on the outcome. The two lines were joined in Utah when the very last spike, made of gold, was driven in with a silver hammer. It was a great day.

The new railroad opened up the West. People now knew that the land they had thought of as a desert was really the finest farm land. New settlers came from all over Europe to homestead in what was to become the great wheat and corn belt of our country. Big industrial towns grew up, using the railroad to ship their freight. These changes and many others came about because of the brave men who laid eighteen hundred miles of track through a wilderness. They made it possible to cross America by rail, from sea to shining sea.

QUESTIONS
---

1. How did the Pacific railroad help America grow?
2. Find a map that shows the route of the Pacific railroad.
3. Find out more about the Iron Horse and railroad people. Who was John Henry? Casey Jones?
4. Find some railroad work songs.

Drill Ye Tarriers

Railroad Work Song

Ev'ry mornin' at seven o'clock,
There were twenty tarriers a-drillin' on the rock,
And the boss comes around, and he says, "Keep still!
Come down heavy on the cast iron drill;
And drill, ye Tarriers, drill!
And drill, ye Tarriers, drill!
For it's work all day for sugar in your tay,
Down behind the railway,
And drill, ye Tarriers, drill!"

Part Two

Stories and Poems
Everyone Likes

The Real Princess

Hans Christian Andersen

A long time ago there was a prince who wanted to marry a princess—but she had to be a *real* princess. He traveled all over the world looking for one.

There were many princesses, but there was always something about them that was not quite right. At last the prince had to give up, and he returned to his castle. He was sad because he wanted a *real* princess very much.

One night there was a terrible storm. The lightning flashed, the thunder roared, and the rain came down in torrents. It was a fearful night. Suddenly a knock was heard on the castle gate. The old king himself went down to see who it was.

There, standing outside in the rain, stood a princess. She didn't look like a princess because her hair and clothes were soaking wet and water was streaming out of her shoes.

"I am a princess," she said. "May I find shelter here tonight?"

The king kindly invited her in, and then he went to tell the queen.

"We will soon see if she is a real princess," said the queen to herself. She went into a room to get a bed ready for the

---

WORDS TO WATCH

| torrents | mattress | museum |

princess. She took all the bedclothes off the bed and laid a pea on the bedstead. Then she took twenty mattresses and put them on top of the pea. Then on top of the mattresses, she piled twenty feather beds. The princess was to sleep on top of all these mattresses and feather beds.

The next morning the queen asked her if she had slept well.

"It was terrible," said the princess. "I hardly closed my eyes the whole night. Heaven knows what was in the bed. I was lying on something so hard that I am black and blue all over."

When the queen heard this, she knew the girl was a *real* princess, for only a *real* princess could feel a pea through twenty mattresses and twenty feather beds.

The prince was overjoyed to find a real princess. He took her for his wife the very next day, and the pea was put into a museum for everyone to see.

QUESTIONS

1. Why was the prince sad?
2. How did the queen test the girl to see if she was a real princess?
3. What did the princess say when the queen asked her if she had slept well?
4. What happened after the prince found out that the princess was a real princess?

The Tardy Teacher

Edward Eggleston

In the schools of long ago, a student who did not behave in class was beaten by the teacher with a switch or a stick. The teacher hit the student hard enough so that it really hurt. But in the city of Philadelphia before the Revolutionary War, there was a teacher named Mr. Dove who did not beat his students.

When a boy behaved badly in class, Mr. Dove would not beat him with a switch. Instead, he would stick the switch into the back of the boy's coat collar so that it would rise in the air above his head. Then the boy had to stand up on a

---

WORDS TO WATCH

| behave | Revolutionary War | ashamed |
| Philadelphia | Mr. Dove | tardy |

bench in front of the other students and feel ashamed for not behaving himself.

If a student did not come to school on time, Mr. Dove would send five or six boys to bring the tardy student to school. One of these boys would carry a lighted lantern, and another would carry a bell. The tardy student had to march down the street in broad daylight. One of the boys would walk behind him and ring the bell to show that the tardy student should be in school. Another would walk in front of him with the lighted lantern to show him the way.

One morning Mr. Dove himself slept too late. When the boys saw that he did not come to school on time, they took the lighted lantern and the bell and went to his house to get him. They brought him to school with one boy ringing the bell behind him and another boy walking in front of him with the lighted lantern. Mr. Dove told the boys that they were right because everybody should try to be on time no matter who he or she is.

QUESTIONS

1. How did Mr. Dove punish students who did not behave in class?
2. What happened when a boy did not come to school on time?
3. Why was Mr. Dove not angry when the boys came after him to take him to school?

Things to Collect

I. Read and Spell

stamps	plants	autographs
coins	matchbooks	photographs
poems	pictures	stories
insects	flowers	seashells
butterflies	books	rare things
leaves	postcards	anything

II. Read and Answer

1. Which of these things do not cost money to collect?
2. Which of these things do you collect?
3. What would you like most to collect?
4. Name some other things to collect.

III. Write

1. Write five sentences, each using a word in Part I.
2. Write about what you collect or would like to collect.

The Wind and the Sun

Aesop

Once the wind and the sun had a great quarrel. The wind said he was stronger than the sun. The sun said he was stronger than the wind. They wished for some way to see which was the stronger.

Soon a man came along the road.

"See that man," said the wind. "I can make him take off his coat."

"No, you cannot," said the sun, "but I can."

"We will try," they both said.

The wind said he would try first. He blew as hard as he could. What a noise he made!

The man said, "It is very cold." So he did not take off his coat but pulled it tighter around himself.

At last the wind said, "I cannot make the man take off his coat."

Then the sun tried. He made no noise. He shone hotter and hotter.

"How warm it is!" said the man. Then he took off his coat.

"See what I did!" said the sun to the wind. "I made the man take off his coat. I am stronger than you."

Which do you think was the stronger, the wind or the sun?

Good Morning, Merry Sunshine

Anonymous

Good morning, merry sunshine,
How did you wake so soon?
You've scared the little stars away,
And shined away the moon;
I saw you go to sleep last night,
Before I ceased my playing.
How did you get 'way over here,
And where have you been staying?

I never go to sleep, dear;
I just go round to see
My little children of the East
Who rise and watch for me.
I waken all the birds and bees,
And flowers on the way,
And last of all the little child
Who stayed out late to play.

Rumpelstiltskin

Brothers Grimm

There was once a miller who was poor, but he had a beautiful daughter. It happened one day that he came to speak to the king. In order to make himself seem important, he told the king that he had a daughter who could spin gold out of straw. The king said to the miller, "That is an art that pleases me well. If your daughter is as clever as you say, bring her to my castle tomorrow. I will see if she can do as you have told me."

WORDS TO WATCH		
Rumpelstiltskin	astonished	Melchior
spindle	messenger	Balthazar
bobbin	Caspar	seize

When the girl was brought to him, the king led her into a room full of straw, gave her a wheel and spindle, and said, "Now set to work. If by the early morning you have not spun this straw into gold, you shall die." Then he shut the door and left her there alone.

The poor miller's daughter did not know what to do. She had no idea how to spin straw into gold. She was so unhappy that she began to cry. All at once the door opened, and in came a little man.

"Good evening, miller's daughter," he said. "Why are you crying?"

"Oh," answered the girl, "I have to spin gold out of this straw, and I don't know how."

Then the little man said, "What will you give me if I spin it for you?"

"My necklace," said the girl.

The little man took the necklace, seated himself before the wheel, and whirr, whirr, whirr! three times round and the bobbin was full. Then he took up another bunch of straw, and whirr, whirr, whirr! three times round and that was full. And so he went on until the morning. By then all the straw had been spun, all the bobbins were full of gold, and the little man had gone.

At sunrise the king returned. When he saw the gold, he was astonished and overjoyed because he was very greedy. He had the miller's daughter taken into another room filled with straw, much bigger than the last. Again he told her that if she valued her life, she must spin it all into gold in one night. The girl did not know what to do, so she began to cry. Then the door opened, and the little man appeared again and said, "What will you give me if I spin all this straw into gold?"

"The ring from my finger," answered the girl.

So the little man took the ring and began again to send the wheel whirring round. By the next morning, all the straw was spun into glistening gold and the little man had gone. The king rejoiced at the sight. But he could never have enough gold, so he had the miller's daughter taken into a still larger room full of straw. He said, "This, too, must be spun in one night. If you can do it, you shall be my wife." For he thought, "Although she is only a miller's daughter, I am not likely to find anyone richer in the whole world."

As soon as the girl was left alone, the little man appeared for the third time and said, "What will you give me if I spin the straw for you this time?"

"I have nothing left to give," answered the girl.

"Then you must promise me the first child you have after you are queen," said the little man.

"But who knows whether that will happen?" thought the girl. Since she did not know what else to do, she promised the little man what he desired. Then he began to spin until all the straw was gold. When in the morning the king came and found all done according to his wish, he ordered the wedding to be held at once, and the miller's pretty daughter became a queen.

In a year's time she brought a fine child into the world and thought no more of the little man. But one day he came suddenly into her room and said, "Now give me what you promised."

The queen was terrified. She offered the little man all the riches of her kingdom if he would only leave the child. But the little man said, "No, I would rather have something living than all the treasures of the world."

Then the queen began to cry. She cried so hard that the little man took pity on her.

"I will give you three days," said he. "If at the end of that time you cannot tell my name, you must give the child to me."

The queen spent the whole night thinking of all the names that she had ever heard. She sent a messenger through the land to ask far and wide for all the names that could be found. When the little man came the next day, she repeated all the names she knew—like Caspar, Melchior, and Balthazar. She went through the whole list, but after each one the little man said, "That is not my name."

The second day the queen sent to inquire of all the neighbors what their servants were called. She told the little man all the unusual names she could find.

"Perhaps you are Roast-ribs," she said, "or Sheepshanks, or Spindleshanks?" But all he answered was, "That is not my name."

The third day the messenger came back again and said,
"I have not been able to find one single new name, but as I
passed through the woods, I came to a high hill. Near it was a
little house, and before the house burned a fire. Around the
fire danced a funny little man, hopping on one leg and singing,

> 'Today I bake, tomorrow I brew,
> The day after that the queen's child comes in;
> And Oh! I am glad that nobody knew
> That the name I am called is Rumpelstiltskin!' "

You cannot think how pleased the queen was to hear that
name! Soon afterward the little man walked in and asked,
"Now, Mrs. Queen, what is my name?"

"Are you called Jack?" she said at first.

"That is not my name," he answered.

"Are you called Harry?" she asked again.

"That is not my name," he said.

"Then perhaps your name is Rumpelstiltskin!"

"The devil told you that! The devil told you that!" cried the little man, and in his anger he stamped with his right foot so hard that it went into the ground above his knee. Then he seized his left foot with both his hands in such a fury that he split in two, and that was the end of him.

QUESTIONS

1. Why did the miller tell the king that his daughter could spin straw into gold?
2. What did the miller's daughter give Rumpelstiltskin the first time he spun straw into gold? The second time? The third time?
3. When Rumpelstiltskin saw the queen crying and took pity on her, what did he say to her?
4. How did the queen find out what Rumpelstiltskin's name was?
5. Do you feel sorry for Rumpelstiltskin? Why?
6. Which person in this story do you like the least? Why?

Ways to Travel

I. Read and Spell

airplane	train	bus
camel	canoe	streetcar
dog sled	legs	elevator
bicycle	elephant	skis
horse	speedboat	automobile
ocean liner	subway	spaceship

II. Read and Answer

1. Which is the oldest way of traveling?
2. Which is the fastest way of traveling?
3. What is the slowest way of traveling?
4. What way would you like most to travel?
5. What way would you like least to travel?

III. Write

1. Write five sentences, each using a word in Part I.
2. Write a little story about a trip you have taken.

The Adventures of Tom Thumb

English Folk Tale

Once upon a time a powerful magician named Merlin was walking down a hot, dusty road. He had changed himself into a beggar, and he was tired and hungry from walking in the hot sun. Soon he came to a farmhouse. He knocked on the door to ask for some food and a place to rest.

The farmer invited him in. The farmer's good-hearted wife got Merlin a bowl of milk and a plate of brown bread. He thanked them and began to eat. When he had finished his meal, he began to look around the room. He saw that it was neat and comfortable, but he saw, too, that the farmer and his wife were very unhappy.

"You have a pretty little cottage and all you need to live on. Why are you so sad?" asked the magician.

"It is because we have no children," said the woman, with tears in her eyes. "I would be the happiest creature in the world if I had a son, even though he might be no bigger than my husband's thumb."

WORDS TO WATCH		
Merlin	bewitched	apron
beggar	tinker	raven
creature	wringing	swoop
thistle	thread	King Arthur

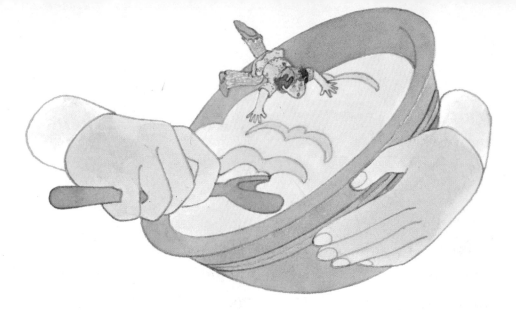

Merlin thought that the idea of a boy no bigger than a man's thumb was very funny.

The next morning Merlin thanked the farmer and his wife for their kindness. Before he left, he said, "You will get your wish."

The farmer and his wife did not know what to think, but soon afterward a son was born to them—and he really was no bigger than a man's thumb.

The queen of the fairies heard about this little boy who was no larger than a man's thumb, and she came to visit him. She kissed him and gave him the name Tom Thumb. Then she ordered her fairies to make him some clothes. They made his hat out of an oak leaf, his shirt of spider webs, his jacket of the down of a thistle, his trousers of feathers, and his shoes from a mouse's skin.

One day Tom was watching his mother making some batter for a pudding. Tom was curious to see how it was made, so he climbed upon the edge of the bowl. Suddenly his foot slipped, and he fell head over heels into the batter. His mother did not notice him. She kept on stirring the batter; then she poured the batter into a pot and set it on the fire to boil.

Tom's mouth filled up with batter so that he couldn't cry out. Soon he began to feel the hot water, and he began kicking and struggling in the pot. His mother thought that the pudding was bewitched, so she took the pot off the stove and threw the pudding outside the door.

Just then a tinker was passing by. He saw the pudding, picked it up, dusted it off, and was just about to eat it. But by now Tom had got his mouth cleared of the batter, and he began to cry out. Tom's cries so frightened the tinker that he dropped the pudding and ran off.

The pudding bowl broke to pieces by the fall, and Tom, who was covered all over with batter, crawled out and ran home.

His mother felt very sorry to see him in such a terrible state. She prepared a bath for him in a teacup and soon washed the batter off him. Then she kissed him and laid him on his bed.

Another day Tom's mother went to milk her cow in the meadow, and she took Tom along with her. There was a strong wind. She tied Tom to a thistle with a piece of thread so that he wouldn't get blown away while she was milking the cow.

But soon the cow spied Tom's oak-leaf hat, which looked

good to eat. So she took in Tom, the thistle, and the thread all in one mouthful. Tom cried out, "Mother! Mother!" as loud as he could, for he knew the cow's teeth would chew him up any minute.

"Tom! Tom! Where are you?" his mother called.

Tom's mother didn't know what to do, so she just stood there wringing her hands and crying. When the cow heard the poor woman making such strange sounds, it opened its mouth, and Tom fell out. His mother caught him in her apron just in time, or he would have been badly hurt from the fall. She ran home with him and tried to comfort him.

Tom's father made Tom a whip out of straw so that he could help drive the cattle. One day as they were walking in the fields, a raven swooped down and snatched Tom up in his beak. Then the raven flew far out over the ocean and dropped him into the water. Almost at once a big fish gobbled up poor Tom. This fish was caught, and when it was opened up in order to be cooked, out jumped Tom, feeling fine and glad to be free once again.

Everyone was amazed to see such a small boy. The people took Tom to the court of King Arthur, and soon he was the favorite of the court.

QUESTIONS

1. How did Tom Thumb get his name?
2. What were his clothes made from?
3. Tell about Tom's adventure with the pudding batter.
4. How did Tom get out of the cow's mouth?
5. How did Tom get to King Arthur's court?

The Horse & the Flea

American Folk Rhyme

A horse and a flea and three blind mice
Sat on a curbstone shooting dice.
The horse he slipped and fell on the flea.
The flea said, "Whoops, there's a horse on me."

Patrick O'Donnell & the Leprechaun

Virginia Haviland

Patrick O'Donnell was coming home one night from the county fair in Donegal. He was taking the rise in the road when he heard off in the bogland a shrill wee cry.

Said he to himself, " 'Tis not the cry of a wee one and 'tis not the cry of a creature caught in the furze. I will go and have a look."

So over the bog he stepped, passing one blackthorn bush after another, for the bog was full of them. And he came at last to the thorn bush that was holding the cry.

Now there was a moon in the sky and the skies were bright, so he could see what was there. He could see to his wonderment a wee fairy man hung by the seat of his breeches on a long black thorn. He stepped closer now and asked, "How did you get yourself in this plight, wee small man that you are?"

With that he knocked his foot on something small on the ground and he looked below. There he saw a wee cobbler's bench with pegs and bits of leather and with all the things of a cobbler's trade.

"Aha," he said aloud to himself and the wee man. " 'Tis a leprechaun you are, wee man."

The leprechaun had stopped his squealing, and now he spoke with great impatience. "It's a small matter if I am. Take me off the blackthorn, where I'm likely to die if you don't. And take great care that you do not tear my breeches, for they are a new pair."

You can well believe that Patrick O'Donnell was filled with more than wonderment now, for he knew that the leprechaun was safe in his hands. He could ask where the crock of fairy gold was hidden, and the leprechaun by all the laws of fairy trade was bound to tell him.

So, with great care, he took the wee man by the scruff of his neck and the seat of his breeches and gently lifted him free of the blackthorn.

"Put me fast to the earth," said the wee man.

"I will not," said Patrick. " 'Tis a leprechaun you are, and 'tis on you I'll keep my hands and my eyes until you'll be after telling me where the pot of gold is hid."

"Have a heart," said the wee man. "What is a pot of gold to you?"

" 'Tis the making of my family fortune," said Patrick O'Donnell, "and without it I am thinking we'll never have one."

There followed a long time with nought but blathering between them. In the end, with his hands still fast on the seat of his breeches and the scruff of his neck, Patrick O'Donnell went across the bog as the leprechaun directed, until they came to a certain blackthorn bush.

" 'Tis here it is hid," said the leprechaun, sounding sad.

"Are you sure?" asked Patrick O'Donnell.

"I'm as sure of it as that I am the wee man who mends all the fairies' shoes after their dancing. Dig under that blackthorn yonder, and you'll find the fairies' gold."

Patrick O'Donnell looked about him under the starlight at all the blackthorn bushes on the bog and he shook his head with great hopelessness.

"I have no spade at all to dig with," said he, "and if I go home for it, how will I find which bush it is when I come back?"

"That's a trouble that's all your own," said the wee fairy man. With that a great silence fell between them.

It was Patrick himself that broke it.

"I have the answer," said he, sending up a great shout. "I'll tie my bright kerchief to the bush, and even by the starlight, dark as it is, I'll be able to tell which bush holds the crock of gold."

The fairy man set up a great chuckling. "Tie your kerchief fast now, and leave us both be going our ways."

Patrick, now sure of his family's fortune, let the leprechaun go. Whisht! Like a shooting star in the night, he vanished, while Patrick untied the kerchief from about his neck and tied it fast to the blackthorn bush.

It took him the rest of the night to reach home and find himself a stout spade, and then tramp down to the bog again.

The bright orange of the sunrise was making a ring for the new day around the sky when he started across the bog. It made bright every patch of grass and stubble, furze and bush, as he tramped.

He was half across the bog when he looked about. To his great bewilderment he saw that every thorn bush around him had a bright kerchief tied to it, the same as he had tied to the thorn bush the leprechaun had shown him.

"If I should live to be a hundred," said Patrick O'Donnell, "I could never dig up the whole of them." So there was the ending of the O'Donnell fortune.

Johnny Appleseed

Joanna Strong and Tom B. Leonard

"Daddy, I want something to eat! Daddy, I'm thirsty!" little Billy and Mary Stover cried, as they sat huddled in the back of the bouncing wagon. The wagon was loaded high with pots and pans and blankets and clothes. The Stover family were pioneers. They were traveling into the unsettled territory of the Middle West, where they were going to build their new home.

"There'll be something to eat and drink in a little while, children," Mr. Stover answered, with a cheerfulness he did not feel. For where, where in this wild land could they expect to find any food? In his heart he was praying for a miracle to help them.

Then suddenly little Billy cried out. "Look, Daddy, look! Apple trees! Over there on the left!" And sure enough, there was a whole orchard of young trees, heavy with fruit, appearing like the miracle Mr. Stover had prayed for.

"This must be the work of Johnny Appleseed," Mr. Stover cried thankfully. "May the Lord bless him to the end of his days."

This was indeed the gift of Johnny Appleseed—the same kind of gift he made to hundreds of other pioneer families like the Stovers. For Johnny Appleseed had set out as a young man, all alone, into the unexplored wilderness, with

a bag of apple seeds over his shoulder. Wherever he found a spot that looked right to him, he planted his seeds and continued on.

For forty-six years he planted this unexpected treasure for other settlers to find. And in all the forty-six years that Johnny Appleseed spent making his way alone in the wilds and forest lands, among bears, wolves, wild hogs, poisonous snakes, and savage Indian tribes, he never carried a gun. He believed that it was a sin to kill any living thing, even a mosquito. And in all that time, no harm ever came to him! The Indians became his friends, and perhaps even the animals could tell that he would not hurt them.

No one knows where Johnny Appleseed finally was laid to rest, but in the spring, when the apple orchards of Pennsylvania, Ohio, and Indiana are in bloom, the deeds of this brave and kindhearted man are brought to mind by the sweet perfume of the apple blossoms.

QUESTIONS
---

1. Where was the Stover family going?
2. How did Johnny Appleseed help the Stover family?
3. What kind of man do you think Johnny Appleseed was? Why?

Sports

I. Read and Spell

fishing	tennis	volleyball
hiking	bowling	swimming
baseball	football	basketball
hockey	hunting	golf
badminton	softball	camping
boating	running	jumping
bicycling	skiing	sledding
soccer	horseback riding	sailing
ice skating	walking	mountain climbing

II. Read and Answer

1. Which of these sports are played by teams?
2. Which sport do you think is the most dangerous?
3. Which sport would you like least?
4. Which sport would you like most to be good at?

III. Write

1. Write five sentences, each one using a word in Part I.
2. Write about the sport you like best.

The Frog Prince
Brothers Grimm

In old times, when you could still wish for what you wanted, there lived a king whose daughters were all handsome. The youngest was so beautiful that the sun himself, who has seen so much, wondered at her beauty. Near the royal castle there was a great dark wood, and in the wood under an old linden tree was a well. When the day was hot, the king's daughter used to go into the wood and sit by the cool well. If the time passed slowly, she took her golden ball, threw it up in the air, and caught it again. That was her favorite game.

WORDS TO WATCH		
handsome	unwilling	plumes
linden tree	heartily	ache
insisted	bridegroom	grieved

One day the golden ball did not fall back to her out-stretched hands, but fell to the ground near the edge of the well and bounced in. The king's daughter followed it with her eyes as it sank, but the well was deep, so deep that she could not see the bottom. Then she began to weep, and she wept and wept as if her heart would break.

As she was weeping, she heard a voice calling, "What's the matter, king's daughter? Your tears break my heart."

She looked to see where the voice came from, but saw only a frog stretching his fat, ugly head out of the water.

"Oh, is it you, old frog?" said she. "I am weeping because my golden ball fell into the well."

"Sh-sh. Don't cry. I'll try to help you. But first, what will you give me if I bring back your ball?"

"Whatever you like, dear frog," she said. "My clothes, my pearls and jewels, or even the gold crown I am wearing."

"Your clothes, pearls and jewels, and your crown of gold are not for me," the frog answered. "But if you would love me and be my friend, let me come and play with you, let me sit by you at the table and eat from your plate and drink from your cup, and let me sleep in your little bed; if you promise me all this, then I will bring back your golden ball."

As soon as she had given her promise to do all that the frog wanted, he disappeared under the water. Then, after a while, he came up with the ball in his mouth and threw it on the grass. The king's daughter was so happy to see her pretty plaything again that she picked it up and ran off with it.

"Wait, wait!" called the frog. "Take me with you, I can't run as fast as you." But for all his quawk, quawk, quawking as loudly as he could, she would not listen. She hurried home and very soon forgot all about the poor frog.

The next day, when the king's daughter was sitting at the table with the king and all the court and was eating from her little golden plate, something came plitch, platch, plitch, platch, up the marble steps. Then there came a knocking at the door and a cry, "King's youngest daughter, let me in!"

She got up and ran to see who it could be. When she opened the door, she saw the frog sitting there. She quickly shut the door and went back to her place at the table, feeling very frightened.

The king noticed how quickly her heart was beating and said, "My child, why are you afraid? Is there a giant standing at the door ready to carry you off?"

"Oh, no," she answered, "it's not a giant, but a horrible frog."

"And what does the frog want?"

"Oh, dear father," answered she, "when I was sitting by the well yesterday playing with my golden ball, it fell into the well. While I was crying over the loss of it, the frog came and got it for me. Only because he insisted, I promised that he could play with me and be my friend. But I never thought he could leave the water. Now he is outside the door, and he wants to come in to play with me and to eat with me."

And then they all heard the frog knocking a second time, and he cried,

> "King's youngest daughter, let me in!
> What has been your promise to me?
> King's youngest daughter,
> Now open to me!"

Then the king said, "You must keep your word if you have promised. Go now and let him in."

She went and opened the door, and the frog hopped in, following at her heels until she reached her chair. Then he stopped and cried, "Lift me up to sit by you." But she waited until the king ordered her. When the frog was on the chair, he wanted to get on the table, and there he sat and said, "Now push your little golden plate a bit nearer so that we can eat together." And so she did, but everyone could see how unwilling she was. The frog ate heartily, but every bite seemed to stick in the king's daughter's throat.

At last he said, "I have had enough. Carry me to your

room and make ready your bed so we can lie down to sleep."

Then the king's daughter began to cry and was afraid of the cold frog, who wanted to sleep in her pretty, clean bed.

The king grew angry with her and said, "What you promised in time of need, you must now carry out."

So she picked up the frog with two fingers and carried him upstairs and put him in a corner. Then when she was lying in bed, he crept up to her, saying, "I am tired and want to sleep. Let me up or I shall tell your father." She was beside herself with rage, picked him up, and threw him against the wall, crying, "Now will you be quiet, you horrid frog?"

But when he fell, he was no longer a frog, but a prince with beautiful, friendly eyes. And with her father's consent, they became bride and bridegroom. He told her how a wicked witch had bewitched him and that no one but her could have saved him from being a frog all his life.

They fell asleep. The next morning when the sun awoke them, a carriage came, drawn by eight white horses with white plumes on their heads and with a golden harness. Behind the carriage was faithful Henry, the prince's servant.

Faithful Henry had been so troubled when his master was turned into a frog that he had to wear three iron bands over his heart to keep it from breaking. Faithful Henry helped the king's youngest daughter and prince into the carriage and got up behind to drive them to their kingdom. He was full of joy that his master had been saved.

When they had gone part of the way, the prince heard something cracking. He turned around and cried, "Isn't something breaking?" Again and once again, the prince thought he heard the same sound.

"They're the bands round my heart
That to lessen its ache
When I grieved for your sake
I bound round my heart."

It was the breaking of the three bands from faithful Henry's heart because he was now so happy.

QUESTIONS

1. When did the king's youngest daughter first see the frog?
2. What did the frog make her promise?
3. Did the young girl want to keep her promise?
4. Did she keep her promise?
5. What happened to the frog?

The Story of Grandpa's Sled and the Pig

Laura Ingalls Wilder

When your Grandpa was a boy, Laura, Sunday did not begin on Sunday morning, as it does now. It began at sundown on Saturday night. Then everyone stopped every kind of work or play.

Supper was solemn. After supper, Grandpa's father read aloud a chapter of the Bible, while everyone sat straight and still in his chair. Then they all knelt down, and their father said a long prayer. When he said, "Amen," they got up from their knees and each took a candle and went to bed. They must go straight to bed, with no playing, laughing, or even talking.

Sunday morning they ate a cold breakfast, because nothing could be cooked on Sunday. Then they all dressed in their best clothes and walked to church. They walked, because hitching up the horses was work, and no work could be done on Sunday.

They must walk slowly and solemnly, looking straight ahead. They must not joke or laugh, or even smile. Grandpa

WORDS TO WATCH		
solemn	catechism	hog
hitching	chores	squeal
fidget	Sabbath	sneaked
motionless	whirr	tanned

and his two brothers walked ahead, and their father and mother walked behind them.

In church, Grandpa and his brothers must sit perfectly still for two long hours and listen to the sermon. They dared not fidget on the hard bench. They dared not swing their feet. They dared not turn their heads to look at the windows or the walls or the ceiling of the church. They must sit perfectly motionless, and never for one instant take their eyes from the preacher.

When church was over, they walked slowly home. They might talk on the way, but they must not talk loudly and they must never laugh or smile. At home they ate a cold dinner which had been cooked the day before. Then all the long afternoon they must sit in a row on a bench and study their catechism, until at last the sun went down and Sunday was over.

Now Grandpa's home was about halfway down the side of a steep hill. The road went from the top of the hill to the bottom, right past the front door, and in winter it was the best place for sliding downhill that you can possibly imagine.

One week Grandpa and his two brothers, James and George, were making a new sled. They worked at it every minute of their playtime. It was the best sled they had ever made, and it was so long that all three of them could sit on it, one behind the other. They planned to finish it in time to slide downhill Saturday afternoon. For every Saturday afternoon they had two or three hours to play.

But that week their father was cutting down trees in the Big Woods. He was working hard and he kept the boys working with him. They did all the morning chores by lantern-light and were hard at work in the wood when the sun came up. They worked till dark, and then there were the chores to do, and after supper they had to go to bed so they could get up early in the morning.

They had no time to work on the sled until Saturday afternoon. Then they worked at it just as fast as they could, but they didn't get it finished till just as the sun went down Saturday night.

After the sun went down, they could not slide downhill, not even once. That would be breaking the Sabbath. So they put the sled in the shed behind the house, to wait until Sunday was over.

All the two long hours in church next day, while they kept their feet still and their eyes on the preacher, they were thinking about the sled. At home while they ate dinner they couldn't think of anything else. After dinner their father sat down to read the Bible, and Grandpa and James and George sat as still as mice on their bench with their catechism. But they were thinking about the sled.

The sun shone brightly and the snow was smooth and glittering on the road; they could see it through the window. It was a perfect day for sliding downhill. They looked at their catechism and they thought about the new sled, and it seemed that Sunday would never end.

After a long time they heard a snore. They looked at their father, and they saw that his head had fallen against the back of his chair and he was fast asleep.

Then James looked at George, and James got up from the bench and tiptoed out of the room through the back door. George looked at Grandpa, and George tiptoed after James. And Grandpa looked fearfully at their father, but on tiptoe he followed George and left their father snoring.

They took their new sled and went quietly up to the top of the hill. They meant to slide down, just once. Then they would put the sled away, and slip back to their bench and the catechism before their father woke up.

James sat in front on the sled, then George, and then Grandpa, because he was the littlest. The sled started, at first slowly, then faster and faster. It was running, flying, down the long steep hill, but the boys dared not shout. They must slide silently past the house without waking their father.

There was no sound except the little whirr of the runners on the snow, and the wind rushing past.

Then just as the sled was swooping toward the house, a big black pig stepped out of the woods. He walked into the middle of the road and stood there.

The sled was going so fast it couldn't be stopped. There wasn't time to turn it. The sled went right under the hog and picked him up. With a squeal he sat down on James, and kept on squealing, long and loud and shrill, "Squee-ee-ee-ee-ee! Squee-ee-ee-ee-ee-ee!"

95

They flashed by the house, the pig sitting in front, then James, then George, then Grandpa, and they saw their father standing in the doorway looking at them. They couldn't stop, they couldn't hide, there was no time to say anything. Down the hill they went, the hog sitting on James and squealing all the way.

At the bottom of the hill they stopped. The hog jumped off James and ran away into the woods, still squealing.

The boys walked slowly and solemnly up the hill. They put the sled away. They sneaked into the house and slipped quietly to their places on the bench. Their father was reading his Bible. He looked up at them without saying a word.

Then he went on reading, and they studied their catechism.

But when the sun went down and the Sabbath day was over, their father took them out to the woodshed and tanned their jackets, first James, then George, then Grandpa.

In the City

I. Read and Spell

street	shopping center	lawns
sidewalk	office	factory
skyscraper	airport	university
train station	city hall	boulevard
apartment house	stop sign	department store
bus	streetcar	subway
traffic	supermarket	streetlight
school	theater	suburb
signal light	power plant	building
zoo	museum	art gallery

II. Read and Answer

1. What can you see in the city that you would never see in the country?
2. How do people travel from place to place in the city?
3. Would you rather live in the city or in the country? Why?

III. Write

1. Write five sentences, each using a word listed in Part I.
2. Write about what you would most like to see in a large city.

I. A. You have read these stories in parts one and two of your book. Tell what each one is about.

How America Was Discovered

The Indians

The Pilgrims

Lewis and Clark

The Great Pacific Railroad

The Tardy Teacher

The Wind and the Sun

Rumpelstiltskin

The Adventures of Tom Thumb

Patrick O'Donnell and the Leprechaun

Johnny Appleseed

The Frog Prince

The Story of Grandpa's Sled and the Pig

B. 1. Which of these stories did you like best? Why?

2. Did you like any of the other stories in parts one and two better than those listed above? Why?

II. A. Which poem in parts one and two did you like best?

B. Copy the poem you liked best; then learn it by heart and recite it to the class.

III. A. Write a story about the character that you liked best in Part One.

B. Write a story about the character that you liked best in Part Two.

Part Three

Famous Americans

Nathan Hale

Nathan Hale was a young teacher when the Revolutionary War began. He believed that the thirteen colonies should be a free country, so he became a soldier in the American army.

During the war, General Washington needed someone to go on a dangerous journey to gather information about the British army. Nathan Hale said that he would go. His friends tried to stop him because they were afraid he would be killed, but he went anyway.

He got the information, but on the way back he was captured by the British. They hanged him because he was a spy. He was only twenty-one years old.

Before he died, he said, "I only regret that I have but one life to lose for my country."

QUESTIONS

1. How did Nathan Hale try to help his country?
2. What did Nathan Hale say before he died?

WORDS TO WATCH

Nathan Hale	information	British
dangerous	regret	anyway
journey		

Benjamin Franklin

One day Benjamin Franklin called his son and said, "William, will you help me with an experiment?"

"How can I help?" asked William. "What are you working on now?"

"I still believe that lightning and electricity are the same, but I want to prove it."

"How can you do that?" William asked.

WORDS TO WATCH

Benjamin Franklin	thunderstorm	Boston
experiment	inventor	Philadelphia
lightning	printing shop	almanac
electricity		haste

"If we fly a kite in the thunderstorm that's coming, maybe we can see an electric spark. If we do, we'll know that the electricity is coming right out of the clouds."

Benjamin Franklin and his son flew their kite in the thunderstorm and attached a metal key to the end of the wire. When the kite flew into a dark cloud, the key made the electric spark which he had hoped for. For the first time an experiment proved that lightning and electricity are the same.

Benjamin Franklin was a famous inventor. He invented a street lamp that made streets brighter at night and a stove that gave more heat with less coal. He invented many other things too.

When Benjamin was only ten years old, he went to work in his father's shop making candles and soap. In his spare time he liked to read and study. When he grew a little older, he worked in his brother's printing shop. But Benjamin and his brother did not get along very well together, so one day he ran away. With a loaf of bread under his arm and a few pennies in his pocket, he went from Boston to Philadelphia.

In Philadelphia he started a printing shop of his own. He wrote a magazine and printed it himself. It is called *Poor Richard's Almanac*. For the next 27 years, he continued to write and print *Poor Richard's Almanac*. It became the most widely read magazine in America. This magazine has many sayings in it that people still use today. Here are some of them.

Early to bed, early to rise
Makes a man healthy, wealthy, and wise.
A penny saved is a penny earned.
Haste makes waste.
Men and melons are hard to know.
The honey is sweet, but the bee has a sting.
Eat to live, not live to eat.
Great talkers, little doers.
Who is strong? He that can conquer his bad habits.

Later Benjamin Franklin was one of the leaders who helped make the United States a free country. In many ways he was one of our greatest people.

QUESTIONS

1. How did Benjamin Franklin discover that lightning is electricity?
2. What jobs did Benjamin have when he was young?
3. What is the name of a famous magazine Benjamin Franklin wrote? What are some of the sayings in it?
4. Why was Benjamin Franklin a great person?
5. Find out more about almanacs.

How Thomas Jefferson Learned

One day Thomas Jefferson was traveling on horseback, and he stopped at a country inn. In the inn he talked with a stranger who was staying there.

After Jefferson left, the stranger asked the innkeeper, "Who is that man? He knew so much about farming that I was sure he was a farmer. Then when he talked about medicine, I thought he was a doctor; and when he talked about religion, I thought he was a minister. What is his name?"

WORDS TO WATCH

Thomas Jefferson	religion	Greek
inn	minister	French
innkeeper	Declaration of Independence	Spanish
medicine	Latin	Italian

"That," replied the innkeeper, "was Thomas Jefferson. He will be a great man some day."

And indeed, Thomas Jefferson did become a great man. He could write so well that he was asked to write the Declaration of Independence. Later, he became one of our greatest presidents.

When Thomas Jefferson was a boy, he liked to play with other boys, but he liked to read too. He wanted very much to learn, and whenever he sat down to rest, he always picked up a book to read.

At school he learned what the other boys did. But Thomas wanted to know much more than he learned in school. He liked to study other languages. When he was a young man, he studied Latin and Greek, and he also knew French and Spanish and Italian.

He did not talk to show off his knowledge. He tried to find out what other people knew. When he talked to a wagon maker, he asked him how to make a wheel. When he talked with the Indians, he asked them about words in their language. By asking and listening and reading, he learned more than most people know all their lives.

QUESTIONS

1. How did Jefferson learn so much?
2. When Jefferson talked with people, what did he do?
3. Do you think Jefferson would have been a great man if he had not read a lot and studied when he was young? Why?

How Many Seconds in a Minute?

Christina Rossetti

How many seconds in a minute?
Sixty, and no more in it.

How many minutes in an hour?
Sixty for sun and shower.

How many hours in a day?
Twenty-four for work and play.

How many days in a week?
Seven, both to hear and speak.

How many weeks in a month?
Four, as the swift moon runn'th.

How many months in a year?
Twelve, the almanac makes clear.

How many years in an age?
One hundred, says the sage.

How many ages in time?
No one knows the rhyme.

The Presidents of the United States

I. Read and Pronounce

George Washington

John Adams

Thomas Jefferson

James Madison

James Monroe

John Quincy Adams

Andrew Jackson

Martin Van Buren

William Henry Harrison

John Tyler

James Polk

Zachary Taylor

Millard Fillmore

Franklin Pierce

James Buchanan

Abraham Lincoln

Andrew Johnson

Ulysses S. Grant

Rutherford B. Hayes

James A. Garfield

Chester A. Arthur

Grover Cleveland

Benjamin Harrison

William McKinley

Theodore Roosevelt

William Howard Taft

Woodrow Wilson

Warren G. Harding

Calvin Coolidge

Herbert Hoover

Franklin D. Roosevelt

Harry S. Truman

Dwight D. Eisenhower

John F. Kennedy

Lyndon B. Johnson

Richard M. Nixon

Gerald R. Ford

James Earl Carter

Ronald W. Reagan

II. Read and Answer

I. Which of the presidents have you heard of before? What do you know about them?

2. How many presidents have we had?

3. How are presidents chosen today?

4. How many years is a president's term?

5. Who was our first president?

6. Who is our president now?

7. Where does the president live?

8. Who is your favorite president? Why?

9. Find out some more about a president you like.

III. Write

1. Write five sentences, each one telling something about a president of the United States.

2. Write a little story about a president you like.

America's First Painter

Benjamin West was the first American painter to become famous. He was born in Pennsylvania and lived with his family in a little stone house when Indians still lived in the nearby woods. That was a long time ago, even before our country was called the United States of America.

Benjamin had never seen a painting in his life, because in those days there were not many pictures in our country. But when he was six years old, he began to draw. One day as he was watching a baby in a cradle, the baby smiled. Benjamin thought the baby was so pretty that he drew a picture of her. The baby's mother liked the picture, so Benjamin drew more and more.

WORDS TO WATCH

Benjamin West	cradle	artist
Pennsylvania	canvas	Philadelphia

He learned to draw pictures of flowers and birds and animals. One day his father found him drawing out in the fields. He was using the red juice of some berries and a stick to draw pictures of the members of his family.

The Indians were pleased when Benjamin drew pictures of them and they sometimes gave Benjamin paints. With these paints he could have more colors in his pictures. He learned that if he mixed red and yellow and blue and black, he could make any color he wanted.

One day he found he could make a better paint brush by taking some long hairs from the tail of his cat. He made so many brushes that the cat's tail began to look bare. Everyone began to wonder what was wrong with the cat.

Benjamin wanted to paint more than anything else. So one day he was given a box of real paints, some good brushes, and some canvas to paint on. This was the happiest day of his life because now he could paint like a real artist.

When Benjamin West grew up, people began to see that some day he would be a great painter. They sent him to art school in Philadelphia, where he studied and learned how to be a real artist. Then one day he went to Europe to study the great paintings there.

In Europe, the king of England heard about Benjamin West. He liked West's paintings so much that he asked him to become a painter at his court. Benjamin West painted 400 pictures and became the most famous painter in England at that time.

Though he never returned to America, he was very generous and helpful to American artists who came to London to study with him. One of these was Gilbert Stuart, who later painted the three famous portraits of George Washington.

But Benjamin West always liked to remember the times when he used to paint with the juice of berries and with the hairs of his cat's tail.

QUESTIONS

1. How old was Benjamin West when he started painting?
2. What were some of the pictures Benjamin West drew when he was young?
3. How did the Indians help Benjamin West with his painting?
4. What was the happiest day of Benjamin West's life?
5. How did Benjamin West become famous after he went to Europe?

Harriet Tubman
Helen Webber

While people were talking about building the great Pacific railroad from east to west across our country, another kind of railroad was running from south to north. It was called the Underground Railroad. But it was not really under the ground, and it was not really a railroad. It was a secret group of people who helped Negro slaves escape to freedom in the North. The home of each member in the group was a "station" on the "railroad." Some members acted as "conductors" to lead the slaves to safety. One of the bravest of these conductors was Harriet Tubman.

Harriet was born a slave, but her spirit was born free. She lived with her parents and ten brothers and sisters in a one-

---

WORDS TO WATCH

| conductors | wound | gourd |
| officers | unconscious | passenger |

113

room cabin with a dirt floor and no windows. When she was only five years old, her owner sent her out to work as a servant. But Harriet did not make a good servant. Her restless desire to be free made her masters angry, and she was often whipped and treated cruelly. Later she worked outdoors where she was happier. Although she was tiny, she worked as well as a grown man in the fields and in the woods. Still, she was known as a troublemaker. And all the while her hatred of slavery grew.

Once she was hit on the head with a heavy weight while helping a slave who was running away. She was unconscious for several days and suffered from this wound for the rest of her life.

Before long, Harriet, too, decided to run away. With the help of a white friend who was a member of the Underground Railroad, Harriet started north. She traveled mostly alone and mostly by night. She knew that to keep from getting lost she must follow the North Star. This is the bright star next to the group of stars that Harriet called the Drinking Gourd. Now most people call it the Big Dipper or the Great Bear.

When Harriet reached the North, where slavery was against the law, she settled down to work and enjoy her new freedom. But soon she risked that freedom to go back to the South and help her sister to escape. Then she knew that this was the work she wanted to do. After that she went south again and again to guide more than two hundred slaves to freedom.

She was called "Moses" because she led her people to a Promised Land. Sometimes she went south dressed as a man and sometimes as a very old woman. Slave owners knew that Moses was stealing slaves out from under their noses, but they could never catch her.

Many other people were fighting slavery at that time along with Harriet. The most famous of these fighters was old John Brown. The old man planned to make war against the slave owners. Harriet helped him get men to join his army. John Brown's plan failed. But then the Civil War broke out—the war that would end slavery in America forever.

During the Civil War, Harriet worked for the North, first as a nurse and later as a scout. With nine men to help her, she explored the countryside at night. The information she gathered was used to help the Northern officers plan their attacks.

After the war was over and all the slaves were free, Harriet went on helping her people. She made a home for the poor and sick among them. But nothing in her long and useful life gave her more happiness than her work with the Underground Railroad. She often used to say, "On my Underground Railroad I never ran my train off the track. And I never lost a passenger."

QUESTIONS

1. Why did Harriet Tubman follow the Drinking Gourd?
2. Was Harriet Tubman a brave woman? Why?
3. Find out more about the Underground Railroad.

Follow the Drinking Gourd

When the sun comes back and the first quail calls,
Follow the drinking gourd;
For the old man is waiting for to carry you to freedom
If you follow the drinking gourd.

The river bank will make a very good road,
The dead trees show you the way;
Left foot, peg foot, traveling on,
Follow the drinking gourd.

Some Famous People of Our Country

I. Read and Pronounce

Frederick Douglass	Helen Keller
Amelia Earhart	Martina Arroyo
Elizabeth Seton	Tsung Dao Lee
Linus Pauling	Henry Ford
Tecumseh	Thomas A. Edison
Charles A. Lindbergh	Mary Cassatt
Mark Twain	Willa Cather
S. I. Hayakawa	John James Audubon
Martin Luther King	Alexander Hamilton
Clara Barton	Albert Einstein
Jim Thorpe	Wilbur and Orville Wright
Eleanor Roosevelt	Jane Addams
Robert E. Lee	Robert Frost
Muhammad Ali	Rachel Carson
Sitting Bull	Chen Ning Yang
Leonard Bernstein	Billy Jean King
Jesse Owens	Beverly Sills
Henry Aaron	Black Elk

II. Read and Answer

1. Find out why ten of these Americans are famous.
2. Which of these people are black leaders?
3. Which of these people are authors?

4. Which of these people are inventors or scientists?
5. Which of these people are athletes?
6. Which person led the South in the Civil War?
7. Which person studied birds?
8. Which persons are Indian chiefs?
9. Which persons are painters?
10. Which persons are musicians?
11. Which person was a nurse?
12. Which of these famous Americans would you like to learn more about? Why?
13. Name some other famous Americans.
14. What makes a person famous?

III. Write

1. Write five sentences, each one telling something about a famous American.
2. Write a little story telling about a famous American you like.

Abraham Lincoln

Some farm boys were talking together in a store in a little town in Indiana. One boy said, "There's something strange about Abe. He's always reading and studying. He reads at night in front of the fireplace, he reads while he is eating, and he even reads while he is resting from plowing in the fields."

"I don't understand him either," said another farm boy. "I heard Abe say once that his best friend was the man who would bring him a book he could read."

"I bet there are more wildcats than books in this part of Indiana," said the first boy.

WORDS TO WATCH

Abraham Lincoln	toddle	borrow
Indiana	Sarah	ruin
Kentucky	husking	

These boys were talking about their friend Abe Lincoln, who worked in the fields with them.

They did not know that Abe Lincoln would grow up to be one of our country's greatest presidents. Neither did anyone else.

Abe Lincoln was born in a log cabin in Kentucky, where his father was a farmer. When Abe was only two years old, he used to help with the farming. He would toddle along behind his father and plant pumpkin seeds.

When Abe was old enough to go to school, he and his sister Sarah had to walk two miles to the schoolhouse. But there were many days when Abe did not go to school. His father wanted him to stay home and do the chores instead.

Abe went to school for only about a year, but he learned to read and write and do simple arithmetic. Most of all he liked to read, and so he read everything he could find.

One day he borrowed a book from a farmer across the way called *The Life of George Washington*. Abe took the book home and read it that very evening. He put it on a shelf high on the wall, but that night rain leaked through the roof and ruined the book. The next day Abe took the book back to the farmer and told him what had happened. Abe said he wanted to work for the farmer until he had paid for the book. So for three days he worked in the farmer's field, husking corn until the book was paid for.

Abe believed in hard work, and he grew up strong and tall. He could chop down a tree or run a farm better than most people.

Once a neighbor woman asked Abe what he wanted to be when he grew up. Abe laughed and said, "I'm going to be president of the United States."

Abe was joking when he said that, but he *did* become president of the United States during one of America's most difficult times—the Civil War, the war between the North and the South. Often during that war, brother was fighting against brother, and father against son.

The Civil War started shortly after Lincoln became president in 1861. Lincoln did what he could to free the Negro slaves and to end slavery in America. Because of his wisdom and leadership during that time, many people believe that he was our greatest president. Five days after the Civil War was over, Abraham Lincoln was shot. He died the following day, April 15, 1865.

QUESTIONS

1. Where was Lincoln born?
2. How long did Lincoln go to school?
3. How did Lincoln show that he thought books are important?
4. What did Abe say when a woman asked him what he wanted to be when he grew up?
5. Find out more about Abraham Lincoln.

Ellis Island: The Golden Door

Judith Barnard

"Come on! Come on!" "This way—come this way!" "Stand here!" "Sit there!" "Welcome to America!"

Every day hundreds of people, thousands of people, stood and sat and moved through the buildings on Ellis Island near New York City. These people came from across the ocean on huge steamships—more than 2,000 people of every age on every ship. They were *immigrants*—people moving from one country to another.

Immigrants came to America to find a better life than they had had in Europe. They came from Russia, Germany, Ireland, Italy, Scandinavia, France, and other countries.

Earlier, blacks from Africa had been forced to come to America as slaves. Later, many immigrants came to get away from unjust rulers. Others came to be free in their religion. But most came because they had been poor in their old countries. They wanted to live better lives.

On a hot July day, Eli and Rosa were among the immigrants, waiting to see their new land. Ahead, a tall, beautiful statue held a torch high in the air. "The Statue of Liberty!" someone shouted. "Ah, *bella, bella,*" (Oh, beautiful, beautiful) said a boy from Italy. "*Eine Riesenfrau!*" (A gigantic woman!) said a German girl. The Statue of Liberty meant freedom and hope.

In 1883, even before the statue was finished, a young immigrant girl named Emma Lazarus wrote a poem about it. In the last line, the statue says, "I lift my lamp beside the golden door!"

What was the golden door? It was not a real door. It was Ellis Island, where the immigrants entered America. Before it was closed in 1954, 16 million people had come through Ellis Island on their way to the cities, towns, and countryside of America.

Eli and Rosa are excited. They can't wait to start their life in America. But first they too must go through the buildings on Ellis Island with their parents and the other 10,000 people who will go through today.

Rosa and Eli have tags pinned to their jackets, with their name and a number. The tags keep them from getting lost.

People are everywhere. They talk and ask questions in all the different languages of their different countries. Rosa and Eli do not know any English yet, only Russian. But they are eager to go to school and learn.

Everyone is told to form a line. Babies are crying, boys and girls are asking questions, mothers are shushing.

Now the line begins to move—slowly, very slowly. Rosa and Eli let someone take their bags and bundles and put them away for a while. Then they move through a doorway to an enormous room, with many doctors in white coats.

The first doctor says something in English. A man next to him says it again in Russian: "Don't be afraid." The man is an *interpreter*. He can speak seven languages! The doctor says, "We're just making sure you're healthy before you begin to live in America. How old are you?"

"Seven," says Rosa. The interpreter says it in English for the doctor.

"Are you here with your family?" the doctor asks. Rosa nods. The doctor watches her. "And where will you live?"

"New York City," says Rosa.

"Good," says the doctor. "You're a bright girl. A fine girl. Go along now."

The next doctor looks carefully at Rosa's hair, her hands, her eyes. He nods. Rosa looks at Eli. "I'm all right," she says. Eli grins. "So am I."

In the last room, men and women with interpreters sit at long tables. Rosa and Eli wait. Their parents are next in line.

"Name?" asks a man.

"Anton Petrovnishkin," says their father.

"Anton Peters. That's your American name." Rosa and Eli are amazed. They have a new name, an American name!

"Do you have money?" the man asks.

"Twenty dollars," replies their father. The man nods.

"A place to live?"

"With my brother," says their father. "He came to America last year. He has room for us."

"A job?" the man continues.

"My brother says I can work in his store."

The man writes in a book. "Is your brother here to meet you?" Their father nods.

"Good," says the man. "Go on, then, Anton Peters. You can live in America. Welcome to America."

Rosa and Eli stand up. They can live in America . . . go to school . . . learn English . . . become Americans! They have come through the golden door.

QUESTIONS

1. America has been called "the great melting pot." Why?
2. Do you know what country your parents, grandparents, or great-grandparents came from? Find out.
3. Write a story about coming to America for the first time.
4. Find out more about the Statue of Liberty.

Part Four

Our Country Today

Our Capital

Every country has a capital, where its rulers live. In old countries, when there were kings, the capital was wherever the king wanted it to be. But when the United States became an independent country, it was no longer ruled by a king. The American people had to decide which of their cities, like Boston, Philadelphia, or New York, would be their capital. Since they couldn't agree, they built a new city, which they named after our first president. The new city had a special state all to itself, called the District of Columbia, or D.C. for short.

The Capitol Building is the most important building in Washington. It is easy to find because of its huge dome and because it sits on a hill overlooking the city. Here the representatives of the American people meet and make laws by which all Americans must live. The representatives, meeting together, are called the Congress.

WORDS TO WATCH

White House	Potomac River	representative
dome	Jefferson Memorial	government
Congress	Lincoln Memorial	Supreme Court
Washington	columns	District of Columbia
Monument	capital	Capitol Building

The most important person in the government of America is the president. The president lives in the White House, which is a large white building surrounded by beautiful gardens. There you can see paintings and gifts and furniture left by many of our presidents. In the garden, each president has planted a tree. Many of these trees are still alive, and you can see them if you visit the White House.

In the Supreme Court Building sit the nine judges of the Supreme Court. They decide whether the laws made by Congress agree with the Constitution. They also decide which side is right in an argument between two people when other courts in the country cannot agree on a decision. The Supreme Court's decision is final.

One of the tallest buildings in Washington is the Washington Monument. From the top you can get a good view of the whole city. Nearby you will see the Jefferson Memorial, a handsome white building on the shore of the Potomac River.

You can also see the Lincoln Memorial, which is made of white marble. It has thirty-six columns, because our country had thirty-six states when President Lincoln died in 1865. Inside, there is a famous statue of Lincoln, the president who declared the slaves in America free. A painting on the wall shows the Angel of Truth cutting the chains that bind a slave.

These memorials were built to remind us of our most famous presidents and what they did. Washington is full of interesting things to see; perhaps some day you can go there and see them yourself.

QUESTIONS

1. Why is the Capitol Building important?
2. What does the Supreme Court do?
3. Which building in Washington would you most like to visit? Why?
4. Find out what the capitals of some other countries are. What are some of their famous buildings and memorials?

Thurgood Marshall

Forrest L. Ingram

"Thurgood Marshall!" the teacher said. "Stop that!"

Thurgood was just about to throw another spitball. "Ma'am?" he said. He tried to look innocent.

"How come your parents call you Thorough-Good, when you're so Thorough-Bad?" She gave him a small book. "You just march yourself down to the basement," she said, "and memorize this page from the Constitution of the United States."

"The Constitution?" Thurgood asked.

"Yes," she replied. "That's the rules people are supposed to live by in this country."

WORDS TO WATCH		
Constitution	Supreme Court	balcony
civil rights	separate	lawyer
slavery	streetcars	usher

Thurgood took the book and went to the basement. He turned to the part the teacher had marked and started reading. The words made him think about his parents, and about his great-grandfather who came to America as a slave many years before.

Most black people who came to America in early times did not come of their own free will. Slave traders took them from Africa and sold them in America to work for white masters.

During the War Between the States, President Lincoln put an end to slavery in America. But black people still did not have much freedom, even in the North.

When Thurgood Marshall was a little boy, black people could not eat in white restaurants. Unfair laws in some states forced blacks to ride in the back of streetcars and trains. Most blacks could not buy a house where they wanted, or get a good education, or a good job. In some places, they were even refused the right to vote given them by the Constitution.

One day, Marshall went to a movie with some black friends. The woman who sold them the tickets told them they would have to sit in the balcony. Blacks were not allowed downstairs.

But Marshall and his friends did not go up to the balcony. They sat downstairs. Soon an usher came up to them. "You can't sit down here," he said. "It's against the rule."

Marshall knew that the Constitution was a bigger rule —the rule that the people of this country should live by. So he and his friends stayed. At last, the usher went away.

Marshall wanted to do something about the way blacks were still being treated in America. He studied law for several years to become a lawyer.

Sometimes people get in an argument about what the law says they can or can't do. A lawyer is a man or woman who helps people with their side of an argument. Often, the lawyer argues their side in a courtroom, before a judge. The judge decides who is right and who is wrong.

Marshall spent a lot of time studying the Constitution. In that school basement many years before, he had memorized the Constitution because he had been bad. Now he studied it in order to do good.

In court, Marshall took the side of many black people who wanted to do things the Constitution said they had a right to do. One day, a young black man came to him for help. He wanted to study law in his home state, Maryland. But there were no law schools there for blacks. The young man wanted to go to school where only whites had gone before. But the leaders of the school refused to have him. Marshall took the young man's side in court. He argued so well that the judge said: "Yes, this man has a right to study in the white school! The school *must* let him in."

Marshall hoped that, one day, black children and white children could go to school together. He brought before the Supreme Court an important argument on that very point.

The Supreme Court is the most powerful court in our land. The nine judges of the Court decide what the Constitution means. They tell all Americans what it allows and what it does not allow.

The people who argued against Marshall said that the states could make laws to keep black children and white children in separate schools. Marshall said that any law which forced black children to go to separate schools was against the Constitution.

The judges agreed with Marshall. In 1954, the Supreme Court said it is against the law to force black children to go to all-black schools.

With the help of the Constitution, Marshall won for black people in America many rights which some states had taken away from them. That's why people call him "Mr. Civil Rights."

In 1967, the president of the United States picked Marshall himself to be one of the nine judges on the Supreme Court. Mr. Marshall is the first black American ever to be named to that powerful Court.

Thurgood Marshall has come a long way—from a school basement to the Supreme Court. As a judge, he works to make sure all people receive fair treatment, as the Constitution says people should.

When Thurgood Marshall enters the Supreme Court building, he passes beneath these words cut in stone: "EQUAL JUSTICE UNDER LAW." The words are there because they say what the Supreme Court stands for. But they also sum up the aim of Thurgood Marshall's life.

THE AMERICAN FLAG

One day Betsy Ross heard a knock at the door of her little shop in Philadelphia. Her uncle, General Ross, and George Washington were at the door.

"Could you make us something special?" they asked. "We want a flag for our thirteen colonies."

"A flag?" Betsy answered. "I have never made a flag before, but I will gladly try. What should it look like?"

"We had an idea that it should have thirteen stars and thirteen stripes. Like this." Then the men drew a little picture of what they had in mind. The stars they drew were six-pointed.

"But," Betsy said, "the stars would be easier to make with five points."

"We thought it would be simpler with six points, like two triangles fitted together."

"Let me show you," Betsy said. She cut out a five-pointed star with one snip of her scissors. The men liked the way she made the star, and so Betsy Ross made the first American flag.

Every country in the world has its own flag. The flag of our country has many names. Some call it the Stars and Stripes. Some call it Old Glory. Some call it the Red, White, and Blue. But most people call it the American Flag.

If you look closely at the American flag, you will see that it has fifty stars and thirteen stripes. Seven of the stripes are red, and six are white. Each star stands for one of the fifty states in the United States. Each of the thirteen stripes stands for one of the first thirteen states, because when the United States became a nation, it had only thirteen states.

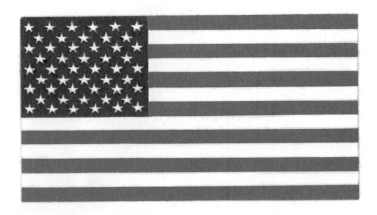

Our flag did not always look the same way it does now. When Betsy Ross made the first American flag, it looked like this:

As each state was added to our country, one more star was added to our flag. Over 100 years ago, at the time of the Civil War, our flag looked like this:

It had thirty-five stars because there were thirty-five states in the United States in 1863.

For a long time the American flag had forty-eight stars. Then two new states, Alaska and Hawaii, were added to the United States. Now there are fifty stars in our flag.

We have a custom of flying the flag mostly in the daytime. It is raised on the flagpole in the morning after the sun is up, and it is lowered at sunset. You can see many American flags flying on holidays such as Independence Day (the Fourth of July) and Memorial Day (May 30). Our flag also has a special day of its own. It is called Flag Day, which is June 14.

We fly the American flag because that is one way of showing that we love our country.

Susan B. Anthony

"Freedom Has a Good Sound"

Judith Barnard

I.

In a horse-drawn carriage, Susan B. Anthony rode from town to town. She was asking people to sign the papers she carried. The papers were petitions. They asked the government to pass new laws to help women. When people signed the petitions, it meant *they* were asking the government for new laws for women.

WORDS TO WATCH		
petitions	articles	suffrage
citizens	juries	factories
opportunity	divorce	elections
federal	amendment	national
approve		abridged

Why did Susan ask people to sign petitions? Because at that time, in 1854, women did not have the same rights as men. Women were not equal citizens of the United States.

In the 1800s, people believed that girls belonged to their fathers. When they married, they belonged to their husbands. If a woman earned any money, she had to give it to her father or husband. Women could not vote in elections. They could not be senators, judges, or governors. They could not be on juries. If they were divorced, their children could be taken away from them.

Susan Anthony had been a teacher in Rochester, New York. She had wanted to be director of her school. But women were not allowed to be directors. Angry and unhappy, Susan left the school. She began to think about what she could do to help women have the same chances as men.

Other women were thinking the same thing. Many of these women were already working together to end slavery. One day, one of the women said: "We don't want black people to be slaves, to be *owned* by white people. But we women live as if we were *owned* by men. If we want *slaves* to be free, we should work so that *women* can be free too!"

The idea whizzed from house to house, from one city to another. "Why not? Why not?" the women said. Suddenly, all over the country, women asked questions about the way they lived. "Freedom," they said. It had a good sound.

Four women became leaders in the long, long struggle for equality. They were: Lucretia Mott, a minister of the Quaker religion; Lucy Stone, a famous speaker; Elizabeth Stanton, who wrote many books and magazines about women's equality; and Susan Anthony.

Susan was a tireless leader. She found women to take petitions from town to town. She found women who would

give speeches in churches and meeting halls and in parks. She ran a newspaper called *The Revolution,* and wrote articles telling about women everywhere in the United States who were working for equality.

At the same time, great changes were taking place in the United States. The Civil War had been fought between the

Northern states and the Southern states. The North had won. The slaves in the South had been set free.

New machines were being invented; new factories were being built. People came from other countries to work in the factories. They called America "the land of opportunity" because everyone in America had a chance for a job. Men worked, and so did women. All of a sudden, hundreds, then thousands, of women were earning money. They were not willing to give their money to their husbands and fathers. "We came to America to be *free*," they said.

Huge meetings were held. So many women came, they could not all get in. They would stand in the street trying to hear the speeches.

Susan Anthony watched what was happening. She decided it was time to form a national group to bring together all the women working for equality. Some of these women were immigrants who could hardly speak English. Others were women whose families had been in America for a hundred years. Some women were rich; most were poor. Some were factory workers; others were housewives and farm wives. The women lived in big cities and small towns. They did not know each other, but they had a common goal.

In 1869, Susan and her friend Elizabeth Stanton began the National Woman Suffrage Association. Suffrage means "the right to vote." The new group was working for many things besides the vote, but Susan and Elizabeth had decided this: If women could vote in elections, *they* could make new laws for women without waiting for men to do it for them. So they worked hardest to get women the right to vote.

Many people laughed at them. Others were angry. "We like men to take care of us," said some women. Men said, "We like women to stay quietly at home and make a good place for us to live." Other men said: "Women don't know anything about politics. They *shouldn't* vote." Many men, and women too, said: "Women belong at home. Men go to work. Women keep house and cook and have children. That's where they belong."

But the United States was changing so fast that no one was quite sure *where* women belonged. Women were nurses. They worked in offices and factories. They were artists. Some ran their own newspapers. Most women still stayed home and cooked and took care of their families. But even these women were beginning to think they should be able to vote. After all, this was *their* country too. Why shouldn't they be able to decide who would be president?

II.

In 1869 Wyoming was not yet a state, but it still passed laws for its people. The newest law said, "Every woman of the age of twenty-one years, residing in the Territory, may . . . cast her vote; and . . . hold office. . . ."

Wyoming was a rough, tough place then, and not many people paid much attention to what went on there. But now they did. Women could vote in Wyoming! Women could run for governor! Women could be on juries in Wyoming!

In the next year, the territory of Utah followed Wyoming. In the West, at least, women were becoming equal.

In New York, Susan Anthony heard about Wyoming and Utah. This was a wonderful thing! But she knew that women could not become equal one place at a time. It was too slow. She knew that the *federal* government in Washington, the government of the whole country, should pass a law giving women the right to vote in every state.

Susan tried for many years to be heard in Washington. Finally, in 1878, a United States senator who believed in women's equality stood up in the Senate. He asked the Senate to vote on an amendment—a new law to be added to the Constitution of the United States.

The amendment had been written by Susan Anthony. It became known as the Anthony Amendment. It read: "The right of citizens of the United States to vote shall not be denied or abridged by the United States or any state on account of sex."

The Senate did not approve the amendment. Most of the senators laughed and went about their business. But each year some senator would try again. Over and over, the Anthony Amendment was brought to the Senate. And each year a few more senators nodded.

And all this time women were parading in the streets with signs. They were marching in front of the White House in Washington. They were taking new petitions from house to house and making speeches and writing articles.

But Susan Anthony was no longer with them. She was old now, and very tired. All her life she had traveled in heat and freezing cold, not having enough money to eat properly, never resting or letting other people do the work for her. Now younger women took over.

When she died in 1906 people said: "She changed America. Once we asked: Will women vote? Now we ask: *When* will women vote? Susan did that for us."

If you open your copy of the Constitution of the United States, and find the amendments, you'll come to the Nineteenth Amendment. It says: "The right of citizens of the United States to vote shall not be denied or abridged by the United States or any state on account of sex."

It is the Anthony Amendment. Not one word was changed from the day Susan wrote it in 1878 to the day in 1920 when it became the law of the land.

Susan did not live to see the amendment become part of the Constitution. But she knew, before she died, that it would be passed—because of the great force that she and her friends had begun to make women truly equal citizens in America.

QUESTIONS

1. How did Susan Anthony and her friends try to gain equality for women in the United States?
2. Why is being able to vote in elections important?
3. Find out how an amendment becomes part of the Constitution of the United States.

THE FIRST AMERICAN IN ORBIT

One February day, early in the morning, John Glenn climbed into his space capsule called *Friendship 7* at Cape Canaveral in Florida.

WORDS TO WATCH		
John Glenn	Florida	orbit
space capsule	Atlas rocket	test pilot
Friendship 7	Mississippi Delta	astronaut
Cape Canaveral	retrorockets	outer space

After much preparation, the Atlas rocket, which was to take John Glenn far out into space, was ready. Soon a voice could be heard: ". . . six, five, four, three, two, one, zero. We're under way!"

The rocket lifted smoothly into the air. Higher and higher it rose until people watching it from the ground could no longer see it. In five minutes' time, John Glenn was 100 miles up in the air, and his space capsule was entering its orbit around the earth. He was traveling so fast that he circled the earth in less than an hour and a half.

Once while he was passing over the United States, he said, "I can see the whole state of Florida laid out just like a map. It's beautiful. And I can see clear back to the Mississippi Delta."

Toward the end of the third orbit, the retrorockets fired, and John Glenn's spaceship began to slow down and return to earth. Soon his ship landed in the water, and then he was safe. And so ended the trip of the first American to orbit the earth.

When John Glenn was a boy, he lived in a little town in Ohio. He liked to swim in a nearby creek and to hunt rabbits. He also liked football, baseball, and music.

He studied hard in school because he wanted to become an airplane pilot. After he had fought in two wars, he became a test pilot.

But he wanted most of all to be an astronaut. He wanted to rise up into the sky to see what it is like hundreds of miles above the earth, traveling 18,000 miles per hour.

Finally he was chosen to be one of our first astronauts because of his good record. But he had to work hard to learn how to handle all the controls in the space capsule.

After John Glenn had orbited the earth in *Friendship 7*, everyone knew what a great thing he had done. People cheered wildly as they saw him pass by in parades.

The president of the United States honored John Glenn too. "This is a new ocean," he said, "and I believe we must sail on it."

It takes brave people to sail on the ocean of outer space. John Glenn, and all those who helped John Glenn, are some of these brave people.

QUESTIONS
---

1. What did John Glenn like to do when he was a boy?
2. What did he do before he became an astronaut?
3. How long did it take John Glenn to orbit the earth in his capsule?
4. Find Florida and the Mississippi Delta on the map on page 164 of your book.
5. How did John Glenn get back to earth?
6. What did the president of the United States mean when he said, "We must sail on this new ocean"?
7. Find out who was the first person in space.

Roberto Clemente

Judith Barnard

Did you ever think about being two people? When you're in school or playing ball or talking to friends, that's the *public* you that lots of people see. But you also do things quietly. You help a friend in trouble. You do a favor for your mother. You share a piece of special cake. That's the *private* you that you don't talk about to everyone.

WORDS TO WATCH

Roberto Clemente	Puerto Rico	league
Nicaragua	championships	Managua
Pittsburgh	webbing	wreckage

Roberto Clemente was two people. In *public* he was one of the greatest baseball players ever. He batted 3,000 hits. His lifetime batting average was .317, and in one World Series he batted .414. He ran so fast that he could beat out an infield hit. Other teams always watched him because he stole so many bases.

Roberto was so good that he won four National League batting championships. He won the National League's Most Valuable Player award once and the Golden Glove award for fielding twelve times.

That was the public Roberto Clemente, the one the fans in Pittsburgh loved and cheered.

And who was the *private* Roberto Clemente? He was the young ball player from Puerto Rico, a stranger in the United States who could barely speak English. He knew what it meant to be lonely and afraid. So he helped others who were lonely and afraid.

Roberto visited sick boys and girls in hospitals. He sent money to poor people. Once, after "Roberto Clemente Night" at the Pittsburgh Pirates' stadium, he was given a $6,000 check. He sent it straight to Children's Hospital in Pittsburgh.

Roberto built his parents a new house in Puerto Rico and took his wife and three sons there for visits. The whole family became friends.

In December, 1972, Roberto read about an earthquake in Nicaragua, a country not too far from Puerto Rico. Thousands of people were killed; the capital city, Managua, was like a pile of broken stones.

"They need help," Roberto said. He asked some people to help him collect food and medicine. When all the supplies were together, Roberto went to the airport to help load everything on an airplane. The plane was an old DC-7. It was overloaded with supplies, but Roberto decided to go on the plane to Nicaragua. He wanted to make sure the people got the supplies right away.

So it was the private Roberto Clemente who died on December 31, 1972, when the old plane crashed in the sea. For days, airplanes and helicopters searched for him. Deep sea divers found the plane wreckage in the ocean, but Roberto Clemente was never seen again.

Lots of people remember Roberto. They remember his great catches in the webbing of his glove . . . his sliding into second base on a steal from first . . . his reaching out to hit the ball into the left field stands. But they also remember the private Roberto Clemente who wanted to help people in trouble. That was the way he lived and that was the way he died.

QUESTIONS
---

1. Who was the public Roberto Clemente?
2. Who was the private Roberto Clemente?
3. Is everyone really two people? Are you both a public and a private person? How?

Part Five

For Readers
Brave and Bold

Leontyne Price

In the small town of Laurel, Mississippi, a three-year-old girl sits at her doll's piano, singing. "I'm giving a concert," she tells her mother.

Years later, in the great city of New York, a tall, beautiful woman bows in the center of a stage. Thousands of people are standing up for her, clapping and shouting, "Brava!"

Leontyne Price had grown up to be one of the world's greatest opera singers. (An opera is a play in which the words are sung instead of spoken.)

When Leontyne told her parents that she wanted to study music to be a singer, they looked worried. "It costs so much," they said. "And it's hard for a black opera singer."

"I want to try," said Leontyne firmly. "As long as one person will listen."

Leontyne tried. She took voice lessons and practiced hours every day. Her wonderful voice became strong. It could reach the highest notes or swoop down to dark, low notes.

After college, Leontyne went to New York, to the famous Juilliard School of Music. There she learned to sing all kinds

---

WORDS TO WATCH

Leontyne	sensation	Laurel
Metropolitan	Juilliard	brava
orchestra	audience	State Department

of music in many different languages. She trained her voice to sing high or low, slow or very fast, soft as a whisper or louder than a yell.

When Leontyne was 25, she gave her first concert in Paris, France. The audience was amazed at her singing. Such a voice! It was beautiful.

Little by little, she began to be famous. She sang with orchestras in the United States. The State Department sent her to foreign countries to sing. Her voice became stronger and more beautiful every year. Soon she was singing in all the most important opera houses in Europe. She was on her way to being a star. But still she had not sung at the Metropolitan Opera in New York, and the Metropolitan is the most important opera house of all.

In 1961, the Metropolitan announced that Leontyne Price would sing there for the first time. Music lovers knew it would be an event the world would talk about for a long time to come. Not many black singers had sung there. But those who had heard Leontyne recently were sure that her color would be forgotten the moment she opened her mouth. The honey sound of a great voice works magic.

And so it was. Leontyne created a sensation. Within a few days her picture was in all the papers and on the covers of the weekly magazines. And from that day to this, her name has been a household word wherever people love music.

Once, Leontyne went back to Laurel to sing. She sang with

all her heart. No one wanted her to leave. But she had to—people in all the big cities of the world were waiting to hear her. Still, she did not forget that concert. "For an hour and a half," she said, "we weren't white or black, we were just human beings together." And that was best of all.

QUESTIONS

---

1. Where was Leontyne Price from? Did she ever sing there? When?
2. Where did Leontyne study music? What did she learn?
3. Find out more about the opera and opera singers. Who was Enrico Caruso? Nellie Melba? Giuseppe Verdi? Richard Wagner?

UNCLE SAM

Uncle Sam is not an uncle. He is not even a real person. But Uncle Sam is important because he stands for the United States.

In pictures he is tall and thin. He has a white beard, and he wears a high hat and a long-tailed coat. His clothes are red, white, and blue, like the colors of our flag.

Nobody knows when people first started calling the United States "Uncle Sam." One story tells about a man in Troy, New York, who saw the letters "U.S." on a large package. The letters mean "United States," but the man didn't know that. A friend decided to play a joke on him. He told the man

---

WORDS TO WATCH

| Troy | New York | package |

156

that the letters meant Uncle Sam. There was really someone in Troy whose name was Sam Wilson, and everyone called him Uncle Sam. So the man thought U.S. on the package meant Uncle Sam Wilson.

Some people think that this joke passed from person to person until everyone was calling the United States "Uncle Sam."

Today all over the world, people know that Uncle Sam stands for the United States of America.

QUESTIONS

1. What does Uncle Sam look like?
2. Did Uncle Sam really live?
3. Does he live today?
4. What does it mean when you say, "Uncle Sam *stands* for the United States"?

My First Buffalo Hunt

Chief Standing Bear

I had learned to make arrows and tip them with feathers. I knew how to ride my pony, no matter how fast he would go, and I felt I was brave and did not fear danger. All these things I had learned for just this day when Father would allow me to go with him on a buffalo hunt. It was the day for which every Sioux boy eagerly waited. To ride side by side

WORDS TO WATCH		
arrows	waist	senses
feathers	breechcloth	instructions
Sioux	rawhide	nervous
neighed	holster	fatal
quivers	grazing	arranged
glow	midst	balance

158

with the best hunters of the tribe, to hear the terrible noise of the great herds as they ran, and then to help bring home the kill made this the most thrilling day of any Indian boy's life.

We all knew that the scouts had come in and reported buffalo near and that we must all keep the camp in stillness. Even the horses and dogs were quiet, and all night not a horse neighed and not a dog barked. Quiet was everywhere.

The night before a buffalo hunt was always an exciting night, even though it was quiet in camp. There would be much talk in the tepees around the fires. There would be sharpening of arrows and of knives. New bowstrings would be made, and quivers would be filled with arrows.

It was in the fall of the year, and the evenings were cool as Father and I sat by the fire and talked over the hunt. I was only eight years of age, and I knew that my father did not expect me to get a buffalo at all, but only to try perhaps for a small calf should I be able to get close enough to one. I was greatly excited as I sat and watched Father working in his easy, firm way.

You can picture me, I think, as I sat in the glow of the campfire, my little brown body bare to the waist, watching, listening to my father. My hair hung down my back, and I wore moccasins and breechcloth of buckskin. To my belt was fastened a rawhide holster for my knife, and this night, I remember, I kept it on all night. I went to sleep with my bow in hand to be all the nearer ready in the morning when the start was made.

The next morning the leaders went ahead until they saw the herd of grazing buffalo. Then they stopped and waited for the rest of us to ride up. We all rode slowly up to the herd, which had come together as soon as they saw us. They ran close together, all of them, as if at the command of a leader. We continued riding slowly toward the herd until one of the leaders shouted, "Ho-ka-he!" which means, "Ready, go!" At that command every man started for the herd. I had been listening too, and the minute the hunters started, I rode with them.

Away I went, my little pony putting all he had into the race. It was not long before I lost sight of Father, but I kept going just the same. I threw my blanket back, and the chill of the autumn morning struck my body, but I did not mind. On I went. It was wonderful to race over the ground with all these horsemen about me. There was no shouting, no noise of any kind except the pounding of horses' feet. The herd was now running and had raised a cloud of dust. I felt no fear until we had entered this cloud of dust and I could see nothing about me—only hear the sound of feet. Where was Father? Where was I going? On I rode through the cloud, for I knew I must keep going.

Then all at once I saw that I was in the midst of the buffalo. Their dark bodies were rushing all about me, and their great heads were moving up and down to the sound of their hoofs beating upon the earth. Then I was afraid, and I leaned close down upon my little pony's body and clutched him tightly. I can never tell you how I felt toward my pony at that moment. All thought of shooting had left my mind. I was filled with fear. In a moment or so, my senses became clearer and I could hear other sounds beside the clatter of feet. I could hear a shot now and then, and I could see the buffalo beginning to break up into small bunches. I could not see my father nor any of the others yet, but I was not so frightened any more.

I let my pony run. The buffalo looked too large for me to tackle anyway, so I just kept going. The buffalo became more and more scattered. Pretty soon I saw a young calf that looked about my size. I remembered now what Father had told me the night before as we sat about the fire. Those instructions were important for me to follow now. I wanted to try for that young buffalo calf.

I was still back of the calf, unable to get alongside of him. I was eager to get a shot, yet afraid to try. I was still very nervous. While my pony was making all speed to come alongside, I tried a shot, and to my surprise, my arrow landed. My second arrow glanced along the back of the animal and sped on between the horns, making only a slight wound.

My third arrow hit a spot that made the running beast slow up. I shot a fourth arrow, and though it, too, landed, it was not a fatal wound. It seemed to me it was taking a lot of shots, and I was not proud of my marksmanship. I was glad, however, to see the animal going slower, and I knew that one more shot would make me a hunter. My horse seemed to know his own importance. His ears stood straight forward, and it was not necessary for me to urge him to get closer to the buffalo.

I was soon by the side of the buffalo, and one more shot brought the chase to an end. I jumped from my pony and stood by my fallen buffalo. I looked all around wishing that the world could see. But I was alone. . . .

I was wondering what to do when I heard my father's voice calling, "Toki-i-la-la-hu-wo," "Where are you?" I quickly jumped on my pony and rode to the top of a little hill near by. Father saw me and came to me at once. He was so pleased to see me and glad to know that I was safe. As he came up, I said as calmly as I could, "Father, I have killed a buffalo." His smile changed to surprise, and he asked me where my buffalo was. I pointed to it, and we rode over to where it lay.

Father set to work to skin it for me. I had watched him do this many times and knew perfectly well how to do it myself, but I could not turn the animal over. When the hide was off, Father put it on the pony's back with the hair side next to the pony. On this he arranged the meat so it would balance. Then he covered the meat carefully with the rest of the hide, so no dust would reach it while we traveled home.

Always when arriving home I would run out to play, for I loved to be with the other boys. But this day I stayed close to the tepee so I could hear the nice things that were said about me. It was soon all over camp that I had killed a buffalo.

My father was so proud that he gave away a fine horse. He called an old man to our tepee to cry out the news to the rest of the people in camp.

That ended my first and last buffalo hunt. It lives only in my memory, for the last days of the buffalo are over.

UNITED STATES OF AMERICA

LAND ELEVATIONS

ABOVE 10,000 FT.
5,000 – 10,000 FT.
3,000 – 5,000 FT.
1,000 – 3,000 FT.
500 – 1,000 FT.
0 – 500 FT.

Atlantic Ocean

Gulf of Mexico

Hudson River

Lake Ontario

Lake Erie

Lake Huron

Lake Superior

Lake Michigan

Appalachian Mountains

Ohio River

Wisconsin River

Mississippi River

Missouri River

Arkansas River

Rio Grande

Rocky Mountains

Great Salt Lake

Colorado River

Columbia River

Sierra Nevada Mountains

Pacific Ocean

Bering Sea

Part Six

On Your Own

George Washington's Breakfast

Jean Fritz

George W. Allen was proud of two things.

His name and his birthday.

George was named for George Washington. And he had the same birthday. February 22.

It made him feel almost related, he said.

It made him want to know everything there was to know about George Washington.

Already he knew quite a lot. He knew that Washington was a general and lived in Virginia and was six feet tall and married to Martha and was the first President of the United States.

He knew that Washington rode two horses in the war, Blueskin and Nelson, but Nelson was his favorite because he was so steady in gunfire.

He also knew that Washington once had ten hunting dogs. Their names were: Tipsey, Pompey, Harry, Maiden, Lady, Dutchess, Drunkard, Tru-Love, Mopsy, and Pilot.

Then one day at breakfast George Allen thought of something he didn't know. George's mother and father had gone to work, and his grandmother was frying eggs at the kitchen stove.

"Grandma," George said, "what did George Washington eat for breakfast?"

"Search me," his grandmother said. "That was before my time." She put a plate of fried eggs in front of George. "And don't you expect me to help you find out either."

George's grandmother knew what George was like. When George wanted to find out something, he didn't rest until he found out. He didn't let anyone else rest either. He did just what his grandfather used to do—ask questions, collect books, and pester everyone for answers. And George's grandmother wasn't going to fool around now about breakfasts that were over and done with two hundred years ago. Besides, there was the spring housecleaning to do.

George punctured the two fried eggs on his plate. "Well," he said, "if I find out, will you do one thing for me?"

"What's that?"

"Will you cook me George Washington's breakfast?"

George's grandmother looked at the clock on the kitchen wall. "George," she said, "you'll be late for school."

"But will you?" George insisted. "Will you cook me George Washington's breakfast?"

George's grandmother was still looking at the clock. "I'll cook anything," she said, "as long as you hurry."

After school that day George Allen went to the library.

Miss Willing, the librarian, smiled when she saw him come in the door. "I wonder what that Allen boy wants to know now," she thought.

George walked up to the desk. "Miss Willing," he said, "do you know what George Washington ate for breakfast?"

Miss Willing could hardly remember what *she'd* had for breakfast that morning, but like George, she liked to find out answers.

Together George and Miss Willing went to the encyclopedia and looked under *W*. "Washington, George." The encyclopedia said Washington was born in 1732, married in 1759, elected President in 1789, and died in 1799. It told all about the years when he took trips and fought battles and did other important things. But it didn't say what he did every day. It didn't mention his breakfasts.

Miss Willing took George to the card catalogue where every book in the whole library was written down on a separate card with a number or letter that told where you could find it. George liked opening the little drawers of the catalogue and finding the right drawer and flipping through the cards until he found what he wanted. There were seven books about George Washington. Most of them were in the section of the library marked *B* for Biography.

George picked out four books to take home, and Miss Willing promised that she would look at the rest.

That night after supper George gave his father a book to

read, and he gave his mother a book to read.

"Don't look at me," his grandmother said. "I said I'd cook but I wouldn't look."

So George kept the other two books for himself. All evening George and his mother and father read.

George was very excited when he found out that Washington liked to count things. George liked to count things too. George had counted how many steps there were between his house and the school. And there was Washington back in the 1700's counting steps too! It made George feel more related than ever.

The book said that once Washington figured out that there were 71,000 seeds in a pound of red clover. And 844,800 seeds in a pound of Red River grass.

But there wasn't a word about Washington's breakfasts, and the way George figured it, Washington must have eaten breakfast more than 24,000 times.

Then all at once Mrs. Allen looked up, "Listen to this," she said. "This book says that in Washington's time breakfast in Virginia usually consisted of cold turkey, cold meat, fried hominy, toast, cider, ham, bread and butter, tea, coffee, and chocolate."

George Allen felt his mouth beginning to water. He grinned and looked at his grandmother.

"Humph!" his grandmother scoffed. "Notice the book said what was *usual* in Virginia. Everyone knows George Washington was an unusual man. No telling what he ate."

A little later Mr. Allen looked up from his book. "Guess what?" he said. "It says here that people in Washington's day didn't eat a real breakfast. Instead they had lunch at ten o'clock in the morning."

George Allen's grandmother grinned and looked at George.

"Doesn't mean a thing," George said. "That book's talking about Washington's day. Not about George Washington."

The day the Allens finished reading their four books was a Saturday, a nice, sunny, spring Saturday. George Allen's grandmother took down the curtains to wash. His mother hung the winter clothes outside.

George went back to the library. Miss Willing suggested that they find out what some of George Washington's friends had to say.

First they read from the diary of John Adams, who was the second President of the United States. John Adams wrote that George Washington ruined his teeth when he was a boy by cracking walnuts in his mouth.

Thomas Jefferson, the third President of the United States, wrote that Washington was the best horseman of his age.

General Lafayette, who helped Washington fight the Revolutionary War, wrote that George Washington wore a size 13 shoe and had the biggest hands he'd ever seen. It was said that he could bend a horseshoe with his bare hands.

No one mentioned if George Washington ever ate or not.

Day after day George and his mother and father and Miss Willing read. George's grandmother started to clean the attic.

Then one day Miss Willing said the reading was over. There were no more books in the library about George Washington. Of course there were bigger libraries, she pointed out. George could go to one of them.

But George had a different idea. "We'll go to Washington's home in Mount Vernon, Virginia," he said, "where George Washington's breakfasts were actually cooked."

The next weekend George and Mr. and Mrs. Allen got in the car. They asked George's grandmother to come, but she said, no, she'd cook, but she wouldn't look. Besides, she was glad to get rid of them, she said. She'd have the attic to herself. No one could poke around trying to rescue things that should be thrown out.

On the way to Mount Vernon, George and his mother and father stopped at Washington, D.C. George wanted to go to the Smithsonian Institution, a museum that had all kinds of historical exhibits—log cabins, covered wagons, and glass cases full of old guns and old coins and old knives and old watches.

"You won't find George Washington's breakfast here," Mr. Allen said. "He ate his breakfasts. He didn't put them in a glass case."

George said that in such a big museum a person couldn't tell what he'd find.

He didn't expect to see George Washington himself, and he certainly didn't expect to see him dressed in a curtain. George's father said that Washington was wearing a Roman toga. Not that he had ever worn a Roman toga, but the sculptor thought he'd look nice in it. George wondered if Washington was embarrassed by the toga, but he decided he wasn't. Washington looked calm and rather satisfied,

George thought. As a matter of fact, Washington looked as if he'd just eaten a nice breakfast. But there was no way to tell what the breakfast was. There was nothing in the museum that told about Washington's breakfast.

Still, George did see the uniform that Washington wore on December 23, 1783, when he resigned from the Army. It was a black and tan uniform, and it had white ruffles and brass buttons. Every place George looked there were brass buttons—down the front of the jacket, on the vest, at the back of the neck, on the sleeves and pockets, on the tails of the coat, and at the knees. George walked all around the uniform and counted the buttons. There were 64 brass buttons.

Then George walked back to the statue. "I bet you and I," he said, "are the only ones in the world who ever counted up all those buttons."

At Mount Vernon George and his mother and father went right to the kitchen. They walked on the same path that Washington had walked on, and every time George put his feet down, he thought of Washington's size 13's in the same spot.

The kitchen was in a separate building at the side of the house. It was a large room with a big brick fireplace at one end and brass pots and iron pots and griddles and pans and ladles hanging on the walls. George held his breath. It was at that very fireplace, he told himself, that Washington's breakfasts had been cooked. The food may actually have been in some of those very pots and pans. Suddenly George felt so related to Washington that goose pimples broke out on his arm.

He turned to a guard in uniform standing at the door. "Can you tell me," George said, "what George Washington ate for breakfast?"

The guard spoke as if he were reciting a lesson. "Breakfast was at seven. The guests were served tea and coffee and meat, both cold and boiled."

"And did Washington eat the same breakfast?"

The guard looked confused. "I don't know," he said. "I've only been here eight months."

This wasn't enough for George. Yet it seemed to him that the answer must be in the room itself. Maybe if he closed his eyes, the answer would come.

So George closed his eyes. He waited, and he listened. After a while he thought he heard a little crackling noise at the far end of the room. He guessed it might be the fire coming back in the fireplace. Then outside he heard a dog bark. Pompey, he thought. Or maybe Drunkard.

George squeezed his eyes even tighter and he listened even harder. Then he felt a shadow at the door. There was a very thin, ghosty-sounding whisper. George had to strain to hear it.

"I served the guests," the voice said. "Now you got the general's breakfast ready?"

George was so excited he snapped his eyes open. But there was no fire in the fireplace. There was no one talking. There were no signs of breakfast. He supposed he'd opened his eyes too soon, but when he tried to go back, it was no use. It was all gone. And the guard was giving him a funny look.

On Sunday afternoon George and his father and mother went home. They found George's grandmother and Miss Willing waiting together on the front porch.

"No luck," George reported. He was sorry that everyone was so disappointed, but he thought they should be planning what to do next.

Instead, Mr. Allen put his hand on George's shoulder. "It was a good try, son," he said. "You can't win them all."

"Sometimes there's nothing to do but give up," Mrs. Allen said.

George's grandmother said she guessed in the long run it didn't matter so much what George Washington ate.

George Allen looked at his family in amazement. "*Give up!*" he shouted. "You expect me to give up! George Washington's soldiers were starving, and they didn't give up. They were freezing, and they didn't give up. *What do you think I am?*"

George was so mad he slammed the screen door and

went up to his room. But even upstairs he could hear them talking to Miss Willing about him. George stamped up to the attic. He sat down on the top step. It was quiet here. And very neat. He could see his grandmother had been working.

Next to him was a box filled with things he guessed his grandmother meant to throw away. On top of the box was an old stuffed dog. He remembered that dog. His name was Ginger. One ear was torn now, and the tail was hanging by a thread. Still, he was a good dog. George put him aside.

He looked back in the box. There was a bunch of old Batman comics. It was a good thing he'd come up here, he thought. No one should throw away old comics.

Under the comics George found a book. It was an old book, torn and beat-up looking — probably his grand-father's, he thought. It seemed a shame to throw it away. *The American Oracle*, the book was called, and it was written by the Honorable Samuel Stearns, whoever that was.

George whistled as he turned the pages. This honorable Samuel Stearns thought he knew *everything*. He told you how to choose a wife, how to kill bedbugs, and how to keep from getting bald. He named the birds of North America (140), and he listed all the famous earthquakes since the year 17 (63 earthquakes). Then there was a chapter called "The Character of Washington."

George looked back at the title page where he knew he would find the date that the book was published.

"1791," he read. Samuel Stearns was living at the same time as Washington.

George turned to the chapter on Washington. "Well, Mr. Stearns," George said, "if you know so much, kindly inform me about Washington's breakfast."

"Washington," Mr. Stearns wrote, "raised 7,000 bushels of wheat and 10,000 bushels of corn in one year."

"Okay, okay," George said. "That wasn't the question."

"Washington," Mr. Stearns continued, "is very regular, temperate, and industrious. He rises winter and summer at dawn of day."

"Then what?" George asked.

"He breakfasts about seven," Mr. Stearns wrote, "on—"

Suddenly George let out a whoop. He put the book behind his back and clattered down the steps.

"Grandma!" he shouted. "When did you say you'd cook me George Washington's breakfast?"

"Boy, if you ever find out about that breakfast, I'll cook it right then no matter what time it is."

"Right this minute, for instance?"

"That's what I said."

George grinned. "Grandma," he said, "put on your apron." He brought the book out from behind his back.

"Washington," he read, "breakfasts about seven o'clock on three small Indian hoecakes and as many dishes of tea."

George passed the book around, and he thought he'd never seen people act as happy. All but his grandmother.

"George," she said, "I don't have the slightest idea what an Indian hoecake is."

George went to the dictionary. He looked under *H*. "Hoecake. A cake of cornmeal and water and salt baked before an open fire or in the ashes, originally on a hoe."

George's grandmother put on her apron. "I've cornmeal and water and salt," she said. "I guess I can make some Indian hoecakes."

George's father built a fire in the fireplace.

George's mother filled the kettle with water for the tea.

George said he'd go down to the basement for a hoe, but his grandmother stopped him. "You don't want me to cook these things on a *hoe*, do you?" she asked.

"That's what the dictionary says."

"The dictionary says *originally*. That means when hoecakes first came out. I expect they'd been around quite a while before Washington's time."

George wasn't sure. He wanted to do it right.

"Did you see a hoe in Washington's kitchen?"

George admitted there was no hoe there.

"All right then," his grandmother said. "Did you see any black iron griddles?"

George said that he had.

"That's what we'll use," his grandmother said. She mixed cornmeal and water in a bowl. She added salt. Then she shaped the mixture in her hands to form little cakes.

Everyone sat around the fire to wait for breakfast. Pretty soon the tea kettle began to steam and the hoecakes began to turn a nice golden brown.

Then George's grandmother served George Washington's breakfast.

George took a bite of hoecake. It was pretty good, he thought. He looked at his mother and his father and his grandmother and Miss Willing all eating hoecakes together on a Sunday afternoon. George decided he felt more related to Washington than he'd ever felt in his whole life.

It was as if George Washington were right there at the fireplace with them. And Drunkard at his feet.

There was only one trouble.

When George finished his three small hoecakes and his three cups of tea, he was still hungry. And if he was hungry, he thought, what about Washington? For a man who was six feet tall and the Father of His Country, it seemed like a skimpy breakfast.

"I hope Washington didn't have long to wait until lunch," he said. "I hope he had a nice big lunch to look forward to. A nice big one. I wonder what—"

But George never finished his sentence. His grandmother was standing up.

"George Washington Allen," she cried. "Don't you *dare*!" And she pointed her spatula at him.

"Not today," Miss Willing said. "The library is closed today."

"Okay." George grinned. "Not today."

UNITED STATES OF AMERICA

Atlantic Ocean

Gulf of Mexico

Pacific Ocean

CANADA

MEXICO

States and locations:

MAINE
NEW HAMPSHIRE
VERMONT
Boston
Plymouth
RHODE ISLAND
CONNECTICUT
MASSACHUSETTS
NEW JERSEY
DELAWARE
MARYLAND
Washington D.C.
Jamestown
Saratoga
NEW YORK
New York
PENNSYLVANIA
Philadelphia
WEST VIRGINIA
VIRGINIA
NORTH CAROLINA
SOUTH CAROLINA
FLORIDA
GEORGIA
OHIO
MICHIGAN
Detroit
INDIANA
KENTUCKY
TENNESSEE
ALABAMA
MISSISSIPPI
WISCONSIN
Chicago
ILLINOIS
St. Louis
MISSOURI
ARKANSAS
LOUISIANA
New Orleans
IOWA
MINNESOTA
NORTH DAKOTA
SOUTH DAKOTA
NEBRASKA
Omaha
KANSAS
OKLAHOMA
TEXAS
MONTANA
WYOMING
COLORADO
NEW MEXICO
IDAHO
UTAH
ARIZONA
WASHINGTON
OREGON
NEVADA
CALIFORNIA
Sacramento
San Francisco
Los Angeles

SCALE
0 75 150 225 300
Miles

HAWAII
Honolulu
SCALE
0 75 150
Miles
N

ALASKA
CANADA
Bering Sea
Aleutian Islands
SCALE
0 300 600
Miles
N

N

Glossary

a_, ă_	apple, tan	ea	eat, leap, tea
ā	acorn, table	_ĕa_	head, bread
à	alone, Donna	ee	eel, feet, see
â	air, care	er	herd, her
ä	father, wand	_ew	few, blew
ạ	all, ball	f	far, taffy, off
a_e	ape, bake	g	gas, wiggle, sag
ai_	aim, sail	ġ	gem, giant, gym
àr	calendar	gh_	ghost
är	art, park, car	_gh	though, thought (silent)
au_	author, Paul	h_	hat
aw	awful, lawn, saw	i_, ĭ_	it, sit
_ay	say, day	ī	pilot, pie
b	bat, able, tub	_ï_	babies, machine, *also*
c	cat, cot, cut		onion, savior, familiar
ce	cent, ace	i_e	ice, bite
ch	chest, church	_igh	high, bright
c̄h	chorus, ache	ir	irk, bird, fir
ch̗	chute	j_	jam
ci	cider, decide	k	kite, ankle, ink
_ci_	special	kn_	knife
_ck	tack, sick	l	lamp, wallet, tail
cy	bicycle	_le	table, ample
d	dad	m	man, bump, ham
_dge	edge, judge	_mb	lamb, comb
e_, ĕ_	elf, hen	n	no, tent, sun
ē	equal, me	_ñ_	uncle, anger
ė	moment, loaded	_ng	sing, ring

1. If a word ends in a silent *e,* as in **face,** the silent *e* is not marked. If a word ends in *-ed* pronounced **t,** as in **baked,** or **d,** as in **stayed,** no mark is needed. If the ending *-ed* forms a separate syllable pronounced **ėd,** as in **load'ėd,** the *e* has a dot.

2. If there are two or three vowels in the same syllable and only one is marked, as in **beaū'ty, friĕnd, rōgue,** or **breāk,** all the other vowels in the syllable are silent.

o_, ŏ_	odd, pot	_ti_	nation, station,
ō	go, no, toe		*also* question
ȯ	come, wagon	ṭu	congratulate
ô	off, song	u_, ŭ_	up, bus
oa_	oat, soap	ū	use, cute, *also*
o_e	ode, bone		granulate
oi_	oil, boil	ṳ	truth, true
ŏŏ	book, nook	u̇	nature
o͞o	boot, zoo	ṷ	pull, full
or	order, normal	ur	urge, turn, fur
ȯr	motor, doctor	ūr	cure, pure
ou_	out, hound	v	voice, save
ow	owl, town, cow	w_	will, wash
_ōw	low, throw	wh_	white, what
_oy	boy, toy	wr_	write
p	paper, tap	_x	extra, ax
ph	phone, elephant, graph	_x̲_	exist, example
qu_	quick, queen	y_	yes, yet
r	ram, born, ear	—y	baby, happy (when
s	sun, ask, yes		it is the only
_s̲	toes, hose		vowel in a final
_ş_	vision, confusion		unstressed
sş	fission		syllable)
sh	show, bishop, fish	_y̆_	cymbal
t	tall, sets, bit	_ȳ	cry, sky
th	thick, three	ẏ	zephyr, martyr
th̲	this, feather, bathe	z	zoo, nozzle, buzz
_tch	itch, patch		

3. The Open Court diacritical marks in the Pronunciation Key make it possible to indicate the pronunciation of most unfamiliar words without respelling.

a·bridge′ *v.* To make smaller or shorter; to reduce.

ac′cent *n.* A manner of pronouncing words.

āche *n.* 1. A constant pain. 2. A great wishing or longing for something.

A·las′ka *n.* The forty-ninth state admitted to the United States; the largest state, located in the northwestern part of North America.

al′ma·nac *n.* A calendar that includes information about the weather, tides, moon, sun, stars, holidays, and special events.

a·mend′ment *n.* A change in or addition to a motion, bill, constitution, or so on.

A·mĕr′i·ca *n.* North and South America.

an′ces·tor *n.* A forefather; a parent, grandparent, great-grandparent, or other person that someone is descended from.

anyway (en′y·way) *adv.* In any case; anyhow.

approve (ap·prŭv′) *v.* To be pleased with; to accept.

ā′pron *n.* A garment worn to protect the front of one's clothing.

Ār′nŏld, Ġen′er·al Ben′ė·dict *n.* An American army officer who turned traitor during the Revolutionary War.

ar·rānġe′ *v.* To put in proper order.

ar′rōw *n.* A straight, pointed shaft that is shot from a bow.

är′ti·cle *n.* A story or essay that appears in a newspaper or magazine.

är′tist *n.* A person who paints pictures.

a·shamed′ *adj.* Feeling disgraced; feeling uncomfortable because one has done something wrong or foolish.

a·ston′ished *adj.* Surprised; amazed.

as′trō·naut *n.* A person who travels in space as the pilot or crew member of a spaceship.

Atlantic Ocean (at·lan′tic ō′shan) *n.* The ocean bordered on the west by North and South America and on the east by Europe and Africa.

At′las rock′et *n.* The device used to send John Glenn's space capsule into orbit.

au′dï·ence *n.* A group of listeners or viewers.

bal′ance *v.* To keep things steady; to maintain equal weights.

bal′cō·ny *n.* A seating level above the main floor of a theater.

Bal·thā′zar *n.* A person's name.

ban′jō *n.* A stringed musical instrument popular in country music.

beg′gar *n.* A person who asks for help, money, or food.

bė·have′ *v.* To act, especially to conduct oneself properly.

bel′la *adj.* An Italian word meaning "beautiful."

bė·wil′der·ment *n.* Confusion.

bė·witched′ *adj.* Under a spell.

Big Dip′per *n.* A group of stars shaped like a cup with a long handle (also known as the Great Bear or sometimes as the Drinking Gourd).

black′thorn *n.* In Europe, thorny shrub with white flowers and small plumlike fruit.

bla′ther·ing *n.* Foolish talk, especially in great quantity.

bob′bin *n.* A spool for holding thread.

bog *n.* A swamp; a marsh.

bog′land *n.* A swampy or marshy land.

bor′rōw *v.* To take, with the promise of giving back.

Bôs′tòn *n.* A seaport and the capital of Massachusetts.

bounc′ing *adj.* Striking the ground or other surface and springing back.

brace′lèt *n.* An ornamental band or chain worn around the wrist.

brä′vä *adj.* The Italian word meaning ''well done,'' used to describe a public performance given by a woman.

brave *n.* An American Indian warrior.

brĕast′plate *n.* A piece of armor that covers part or all of the front of the body.

breech′clôth *n.* A small cloth worn around and hanging from the hips; a loincloth.

breeches (britch′es) *n.* Pants; trousers.

Brew′ster, Wil′liàm *n.* The Pilgrim leader at Plymouth colony.

bride′grōom *n.* A man about to be or just married.

Brit′ish *n.* The people of Great Britain.

brŏok *n.* A small stream.

buck′skin *n.* The leather made from the hide of a male deer.

buf′fà·lō *n.* An American bison; a large, shaggy, oxlike animal.

burial (bĕr′ĭ·àl) *adj.* Of or concerning a funeral.

Cal·i·for′nïà *n.* The thirty-first state admitted to the United States; the third largest state, located in the western United States.

Can′à·dà *n.* The large country north of the United States.

Cà·nā′dï·àn set′tle·mènt *n.* Any of the places where pioneers built small villages in Canada.

can′nòn *n.* A large, mounted gun.

canoe (cà·nōō′) *n.* A light, narrow, open boat.

can′vàs *n.* A strong, coarse cloth used in making sails and tents or for doing oil paintings.

Cape Cà·nav′er·àl *n.* The old name of Cape Kennedy, the site of the United States missile-testing center on an island in eastern Florida.

cap′i·tàl *n.* A city that is the center of some activity, especially a city that is the official seat of government for a country, state, or so on.

Cap′i·tòl Buïld′ing *n.* The building in Washington, D.C., used by the Congress of the United States for its sessions.

Cas′pàr *n.* A person's name.

cat′è·chism *n.* A book that gives a summary of the basic beliefs of the Christian religion, often in the form of questions and answers.

cham′pï·òn·ship *n.* The position of being first-place winner in a contest or game.

cheer′ful·nèss *n.* The state of being happy.

chore *n.* A small, routine job.

Chris′tian *n.* A person who believes in the religion based on the teachings of Jesus Christ.

chuck′ling *n.* Laughing in a quiet way.

cir′cle *n.* A ring.

cit′i·zen *n.* A member of a country or nation.

civ′il rights *n.* The rights to personal freedom established by the Constitution and its amendments.

Civ′il War *n.* The war in the United States between the North (the Union) and the South (the Confederacy).

Clärk, Wil′liam *n.* An American explorer who was invited by Meriwether Lewis to help explore the Lousiana Purchase.

Clé·men′te, Rō·bĕr′to *n.* An outstanding baseball player from Puerto Rico who played for the Pittsburgh Pirates and was elected to the Baseball Hall of Fame in 1973.

cob′bler *n.* One who makes or repairs shoes and boots.

col′o·ny *n.* A settlement formed in a new land.

Co·lum′bus, Chris′to·pher *n.* The discoverer of America.

column (col′um) *n.* A round pillar.

con·duc′tor *n.* A person in charge of a train.

Con′gress *n.* In the United States, the branch of government that passes laws; made up of the Senate and the House of Representatives.

conquer (con′ker) *v.* To take over another people; to overcome.

Con·sti·tu′tion *n.* The set of written rules by which the government of the United States is guided.

Cō·rŏ·nä′dō, Fran·cis′cō *n.* A Spanish explorer who went to Mexico in search of riches.

Cortés, Hernando (her·nän′dō cor·tes′) *n.* A Spanish explorer and conqueror of Mexico.

cos′tume *n.* A style of dress particular to a nation, social class, or period of time.

coun′try *n.* A land; a nation.

cov′ered wag′on *n.* A large wagon with a high, curved canvas top, especially a wagon used by the pioneers traveling West.

cra′dle *n.* A rocking bed for a baby.

cra′dle·board *n.* A board on which a papoose was strapped.

cre·āte′ *v.* To make.

crea′ture *n.* A living, moving being, as a person or animal.

crock *n.* A pot or jar made of earthenware or clay.

cus′tom *n.* A habit; a rule.

dān′ger·ous *adj.* Unsafe; harmful.

Dec·la·rā′tion of In·de·pend′ence *n.* A public statement made by the people in the American colonies on July 4, 1776, that they were no longer ruled by England.

deer′skin *n.* The leather made from the hide of a deer.

dis·ap·point′ *v.* To fail to fulfill one's hopes or desires.

Dis′trict of Cō·lum′bi·a *n.* A federal area in the eastern United States, on the Potomac River, containing the country's capital, Washington.

di·vōrce′ *v.* To legally end marriage.

190

dome *n.* A bowl-shaped roof.

Don'e·gạl *n.* A county in the northern part of the Republic of Ireland.

earth *n.* The world; the planet on which we live.

eel *n.* A long, snakelike fish.

Eine Riesenfrau (eī'ne rïe'sen·frou) The German phrase meaning "a gigantic lady."

e·lec'tion *n.* The choosing of a person or persons by vote.

e·lec·tric'i·ty *n.* A kind of power that produces light and heat.

Ellis Island (el'lis ī'lånd) *n.* An island in upper New York Bay that was a United States immigration center.

Eng'lånd *n.* The country located on the southern part of the island of Great Britain.

Eng'lish *n.* The people of the country of England.

Eng'lish·mån *n.* A person from the country of England.

e·nor'mous *adj.* Huge; vast.

e'quål *adj.* Alike in size, number, worth, and so on.

Eur'ope *n.* The continent bordered on the north by the Arctic Ocean, on the east by Asia, on the south by the Mediterranean Sea, and on the west by the Atlantic Ocean; the second-smallest continent.

ex·per'i·ment *n.* A test; a trial.

ex·plor'er *n.* A person who searches, investigates, or breaks new ground.

fac'to·ry *n.* A building in which goods are made or manufactured.

fast to the earth Down on the ground.

fa'tål *adj.* Deadly; causing ruin.

feath'er *n.* One of the fringed growths that covers a bird.

fed'er·ål *adj.* Concerning or belonging to the central government of the United States, rather than to any state or city.

fi'ber *n.* A thread of mineral or vegetable material from which fabrics are made.

fidg'et *v.* To be restless; to fret.

fig'ūre *n.* A shape; an image.

fire'works *n.* Rockets, pinwheels, and other things that make fiery displays when lighted.

Flor'i·då *n.* The twenty-seventh state admitted to the United States; the twenty-second in size, located in the southeastern United States.

France *n.* A large country in western Europe.

Frañk'lin, Ben'jå·min *n.* An American statesman, scientist, and philosopher who confirmed that lightning is electricity and who wrote and published *Poor Richard's Almanac*.

free *adj.* Independent; not under someone else's rule; at liberty.

free'dom *n.* Liberty; independence.

French *n.* The people of the country of France.

French'men *n.* The people of the country of France.

Friend'ship 7 *n.* The spacecraft John Glenn flew during the first manned American space flight.

furze *n.* A low, many-branched, thorny shrub with yellow flowers, common in European wastelands.

Gates, G̣en′er·a̓l Ho̓·ra̅′ti̓o̓ *n.* A British soldier who sided with the colonies during the Revolutionary War and became an American officer.

g̣en′er·o̓us *adj.* Kind; willing to share with others.

G̣er′ma̓·ny *n.* A country in central Europe.

Glenn, John *n.* The first American astronaut to orbit the earth in a spacecraft.

glōw *n.* The light of a fire or lamp.

gōurd *n.* A melonlike fruit that can be dried and used for bottles, bowls, and so on.

g̓ov′ern·me̓nt *n.* The body of people ruling a country.

grāz′ing *adj.* Eating grass.

Greāt Lakes *n.* The five large lakes in the Middle West between Canada and the United States.

Greāt Plains *n.* The flat, treeless land east of the Rocky Mountains and west of the Mississippi River in the United States.

Greāt West *n.* All the land that is west of the Mississippi River in the United States.

Greek *n.* The language of the country of Greece.

griēve *v.* To be sad about something.

guärd *n.* A protector; a defender.

guīde *n.* A person who leads others into unfamiliar places.

Hale, Na̅′tha̓n *n.* An American schoolteacher during revolutionary times who volunteered for a dangerous spy mission and was caught and hanged.

handsome (han′so̓me) *adj.* Good looking; well built.

här·po͞on′ *n.* A barbed spear with an attached rope, thrown by hand or fired from a gun on a ship to capture or kill whales or other large sea animals.

hāste *n.* Speed; quickness.

he̓ad′qua̓r·ters *n.* The main office or center of operations, as for the police, military, or any business.

heärt′i̓·ly *adv.* With enthusiasm.

herd *n.* A large group, especially of animals.

he̓r′ring *n.* An important food fish found in large schools in the North Atlantic Ocean.

hill′o̓ck *n.* A little hill.

hitch *v.* To harness an animal to a vehicle.

hog *n.* A male pig.

hol′i·day *n.* A day of celebration in honor of a person or event.

hōl′ster *n.* A leather case for a gun, worn on the belt or attached to a saddle.

home′ste̓ad *v.* To settle on a piece of land given to a farmer by the government.

husk *v.* To remove the covering of fruits or seeds, as from an ear of corn.

Illinois tribe (il·a̓·noi′ tribe) *n.* One of the groups of Algonquin Indians who once lived in the Middle West of the United States.

im'mi·grant *n.* A person who enters a country to live there.

im·pa'tience *n.* Restlessness; annoyance at delay.

In·de·pend'ence Day *n.* In the United States, a holiday honoring the signing of the Declaration of Independence on July 4, 1776 (also called the Fourth of July).

In'di·a *n.* A country in southern Asia that Christopher Columbus hoped to find.

In'di·an *n.* A Native American.

In·di·an'a *n.* The nineteenth state admitted to the United States; the thirty-eighth in size, located in the Midwest between Illinois and Ohio.

In'dies *n.* A name once used for India and southeast Asia.

in·dus'tri·al *adj.* Having to do with manufacturing and other such businesses.

in·for·ma'tion *n.* Knowledge; news.

inn *n.* A house in which travelers sleep and eat; a hotel.

inn'keep·er *n.* A person who owns or runs an inn.

in·sist' *v.* To demand firmly.

in·struc'tions *n.* Orders; directions.

in·ter'pret·er *n.* A person who translates from one language to another.

in·ven'tor *n.* A person who devises something new.

I'o·wa *n.* The twenty-ninth state admitted to the United States; the twenty-fifth state in size, located in the north-central United States.

Ire'land *n.* A country located on an island west of England.

I'rish *n.* The people of the country of Ireland.

ir'ri·gate *v.* To supply water to dry lands.

Is·a·bel'la *n.* A queen of Spain long ago.

I·tal'ian *n.* The language of the country of Italy.

It'a·ly *n.* A country in southern Europe, shaped like a boot.

Jefferson, Thomas (tom'as jef'fer·son) *n.* The third president of the United States; the writer of the Declaration of Independence.

Jef'fer·son Me·mo'ri·al *n.* A domed building in Washington, D.C., honoring Thomas Jefferson.

Jo'li·et, Lou'is *n.* A Frenchman who explored and mapped the Great Lakes–Mississippi River area.

Jones, Cap'tain Chris'to·pher *n.* The master and quarter-owner of the *Mayflower*.

jour'ney *n.* A trip; a voyage.

Juil'li·ard *n.* A special music school in New York City.

ju'ry *n.* A group of people who hear the evidence in a law case and give a verdict.

keep'ing watch Looking after; guarding.

Ken·tuck'y *n.* The fifteenth state admitted to the United States; the thirty-seventh in size, located in the east-central United States.

ker'chief *n.* A head or neck cloth; a scarf.

ker'nel *n.* A whole seed, as a grain of corn or wheat.

King Är'thur *n.* A legendary king in ancient Britain; the leader of the knights of the Round Table.

knock *n.* A blow; a rap.

language (lañ'gwảġe) *n.* The speech of a person, nation, or race.

Lat'in *n.* The language used by the Romans.

Lau'rel *n.* A city in southwestern Mississippi.

law'yer *n.* One skilled in law and legal work; an attorney-at-law.

lēague *n.* An association of sports teams.

lep're·c̄haun *n.* An Irish fairy or elf.

Lew'is, Mer'ï·we_th_·er *n.* An American explorer who was named by Thomas Jefferson to explore the Louisiana Purchase.

light'ning *n.* A flash of electricity across the sky.

Lincoln, Abraham (ā'brả·ham liñ'còn) *n.* The sixteenth president of the United States; the president during the Civil War.

Lincoln Memorial (liñ'còn mė·mō'rï·ảl) *n.* A stately building in Washington, D.C., honoring Abraham Lincoln.

lin'dèn tree *n.* A shade tree in America and Europe that has fragrant, yellowish white flowers.

lob'ster *n.* An edible shellfish with five pairs of legs and many with two large front claws.

lō·cò·mō'tĭve *n.* A train engine.

lodge *n.* A house; a cabin.

Managua (mä·nä'gwä) *n.* The capital city of Nicaragua.

Marquette, Jacques (zhäk mär·ket') *n.* A French Jesuit missionary who explored and mapped the Great Lakes–Mississippi River area.

mat'trèss *n.* A large, flat, stuffed pad used on or as a bed.

May'flow·er *n.* The ship on which the Pilgrims came to America in 1620.

med'i·cĭne *n.* The science of healing.

Mel'c̄hï·òr *n.* A person's name.

Mė·mō'rï·ảl Day *n.* A day, usually May 30 or the last Monday in May, set aside in most states to honor dead soldiers and sailors.

Mer'lin *n.* The legendary magician and seer from the time of King Arthur.

mesa (mā'sả) *n.* Land that has a flat top and steep rock sides.

mes'sèn·ġer *n.* One who carries information from one place to another.

Met·rò·pol'i·tàn *n.* The Metropolitan Opera in New York City.

Mĕx'i·cō *n.* The country south of the United States.

mï'cả *n.* A mineral that splits into thin, transparent sheets.

Mid'dle West *n.* The north-central part of the United States, including the land between the Rocky Mountains and the Allegheny Mountains north of the Ohio River.

midst *n.* The middle.

min'is·ter *n.* A clergyman; a pastor.

mĭr'ả·cle *n.* A marvelous happening; something beyond what human beings can do.

Mis·sis·sip′pï Del′tȧ *n.* The piece of land at the mouth of the Mississippi River in Louisiana.

moc′cȧ·sin *n.* A soft shoe of deerskin, first made and worn by American Indians.

mon′ster *n.* A fierce, terrifying beast.

mor′tȧr *n.* A mixture of sand, water, and lime that is used like cement to hold stones or bricks together.

Mō′sės *n.* In the Bible, the man who led the people of Israel out of slavery in Egypt and into the Promised Land.

mō′tiȯn·lėss *adj.* Unchanging in position; still; quiet.

mound *n.* A low hill; a heap of soil or stones.

mū·sē′um *n.* A building in which a collection of objects of historical or artistic interest is shown.

mush *n.* A soft cereal made of corn meal.

nā′tiȯn *n.* People who live in the same land, have the same government, and share the same language, culture, and history.

na′tiȯn·ȧl *adj.* Concerning or belonging to a country or nation.

neigh (nā) *v.* To whinny; to make the cry of a horse.

ner′vȯus *adj.* Afraid; timid.

net′tle *n.* A stinging weed.

New Ėng′lȧnd *n.* The northeastern part of the United States.

New York *n.* The eleventh state admitted to the United States; the thirtieth in size, located in the northeastern United States.

Nicaragua (nic·ȧ·rä′gwȧ) *n.* A country in the middle of Central America.

night′in·gale *n.* A small bird that sings mainly at night.

Niña (nï′nya) *n.* One of three ships given by Queen Isabella of Spain to Christopher Columbus.

North A·mĕr′i·cȧ *n.* The continent containing Canada, Greenland, Mexico, and the United States; the third-largest continent.

north·west′ coast The shoreline of the Pacific Ocean along Washington and Oregon in the United States.

nôught *n.* Nothing.

ocean (ō′shȧn) *n.* The great body of salt water that covers most of the earth's surface, or any of its major divisions.

ôf·fï·cer *n.* One who commands in the armed forces or police.

Ō·hï′ō *n.* The seventeenth state admitted to the United States; the thirty-fifth in size, located in the Midwest by Lake Erie.

Ō′mȧ·hạ *n.* A city in eastern Nebraska on the Missouri River.

op·pȯr·tū′ni·ty *n.* A good chance; a favorable time.

op′pȯ·sïte *adj.* Facing; across from.

or′bit *n.* The circular path in which the earth or any heavenly body moves.

or′chės·trȧ *n.* A group of musicians that plays in concerts, operas, plays or at dances.

Or'e·gon *n.* The thirty-third state admitted to the United States; the tenth state in size, located in the northwestern United States.

or'na·ment *n.* A decoration.

out'er space The space beyond the earth's atmosphere.

Pacific Ocean (pa·cif'ic ō'shan) *n.* The ocean between the Americas on the east and Asia and Australia on the west.

pack'age *n.* A bundle; a parcel.

Pah'kee *n.* An American Indian tribe that is part of the Sioux nation (also called Mandan). —*adj.* Of this tribe.

pa·poose' *n.* An American Indian baby.

pas'sen·ger *n.* A traveler on a ship, train, airplane, or so on.

peg *n.* A wooden spike.

Penn·syl·va'ni·a *n.* The second state admitted to the United States; the thirty-third in size, located on the eastern coast of the United States.

per'fume *n.* A pleasing smell; a sweet scent.

pe·ti'tion *n.* A written request to the government.

Phil·a·del'phi·a *n.* A city in southeastern Pennsylvania, on the Delaware River; the site of the signing of the Declaration of Independence.

Pil'grim *n.* One of the settlers of Plymouth Colony in Massachusetts in 1620.

Pin'ta *n.* One of three ships given by Queen Isabella of Spain to Christopher Columbus.

pi·o·neer' *n.* The first, or one of the first, to explore a new land or try a new method.

Pittsburgh (pitts'burg) *n.* A port on the Allegheny and Monongahela rivers in southwestern Pennsylvania, known for its steel industry.

plight *n.* A predicament; a difficult situation; a problem.

plume *n.* A large, colorful feather.

Plym'outh *n.* The area in New England where the *Mayflower* landed in 1620.

Po·ca·hon'tas *n.* An American Indian princess who stopped the killing of Captain John Smith.

poi'son·ous *adj.* Harmful; deadly to living things.

Ponce de Le'on *n.* A Spanish explorer who discovered Florida in his search for the fountain of youth.

po·ta'to *n.* A starchy vegetable.

Po·to'mac Riv'er *n.* A river flowing southeast from the Allegheny Mountains in West Virginia, along the boundary between Maryland and Virginia to the Chesapeake Bay.

Price, Leontyne (lē'on·tēn price) *n.* An American black opera singer.

priest *n.* A minister; a clergyman.

print'ing shop *n.* A place where books and other written materials are put into print.

pris'on·er *n.* A captive.

Prom'ised Land *n.* A place where people can look forward to happiness.

pro·tect' *v.* To shield; to defend.

Pueblo (pweb'lō) *n.* An American Indian tribe that lives in the southwestern United States.

Puerto Rico (pwer′tȯ rï′cō) *n*. An island in the West Indies that is self-governing but is protected by the United States.

pun′ish·mėnt *n*. A penalty; suffering for a bad deed.

quiv′er *n*. A case for holding arrows.

rā′vėn *n*. A large, glossy black bird of the crow family.

raw′hide *adj*. Made from an untanned piece of cattle hide.

rė·gret′ *v*. To be sorry about.

rė·liġ′iȯn *n*. A belief in or concern with powers, principles, or beings that are beyond the physical world.

rĕp·rė·sent′a̓·tĭve *n*. A member of a legislative body, as the United States House of Representatives.

ret′rō·rock·ėt *n*. A small rocket engine that is usually opposite the main engines and is used to slow a craft in flight, change directions, or separate stages.

Rev·ȯ·lū̠′tiȯn·âr·y Wa̠r *n*. The war between England and her American colonies, 1775–1783, by which the colonies won their independence.

right *adj*. Just; true; proper.

roam *v*. To wander; to travel from place to place.

Rôss, Bet′sy *n*. The woman who is said to have made the first American flag.

Rôss, Ġen′er·a̓l Ġeōrġe *n*. An American lawyer who signed the Declaration of Independence.

rū̠′in *v*. To wreck; to destroy.

rū̠le *n*. A government; an authority.

Rum·pėl·stilts′kin *n*. A dwarf in a German folktale who demands a girl's first baby in exchange for spinning straw into gold.

Rus′ṣia̓ *n*. A country in northern Europe and Asia.

Sab′ba̓th *n*. The first day of the week (Sunday) set aside as the day of rest and religious worship by most Christian churches.

Sac′a̓·ja̓·wē·a̓ *n*. An American Indian woman (a Shoshone) who was a guide and interpreter for Meriwether Lewis and William Clark; the name means "Bird Woman."

Sac·ra̓·men′tō *n*. The capital of California, located in the central part of the state.

St. Louis (saint loṵ′is) *n*. A city in Missouri on the Mississippi River.

salmon (sam′ȯn) *n*. An edible fish with pinkish flesh.

San′ta̓ Ma̓·rï′a̓ *n*. The flagship of the three ships given by Queen Isabella of Spain to Christopher Columbus.

Sâr′a̓h *n*. A person's name.

Sar·a̓·tō′ga̓ *n*. A town on the Hudson River in New York where Americans won a battle against the English in the Revolutionary War.

Scan·di·nā′vï·a̓ *n*. The area of Europe that includes Norway, Sweden, Denmark, and sometimes Iceland and the Faroe Islands.

scis′sȯrs *n*. A tool with handles and two blades for cutting.

scruff *n*. The loose skin at the back of the neck.

seal *n.* A fur-bearing sea animal.

sea ser'pent *n.* A large sea animal; a sea snake.

sēize *v.* To grip; to grab.

sen·sā·ṭiȯn *n.* An exciting event.

sense *n.* The ability to see, hear, smell, taste, or feel.

sep'a·rȧte *adj.* Apart; disconnected; distinct.

Serra, Junipero (hōō·nï'pe·rô sĕr'rä) *n.* A Spanish Roman Catholic missionary in California and Mexico.

shärp' shōōt·er *n.* A person who shoots well, especially with a rifle.

Shō·shō'nē *n.* A person from any of several American Indian tribes in the Northwest who speak the Shoshonean language.

Sī·bē'rï·ȧ *n.* A part of northern Russia that goes from the Ural Mountains to the Pacific Ocean.

Sï·ĕr'rȧ Nė·väd'ȧ *n.* A mountain range in eastern California.

Sioux (sōō) *adj.* Concerning or belonging to the Sioux, an American Indian tribe.

slāv'er·y *n.* The practice in which one person owns another.

Smith, Cap'tȧin John *n.* An early explorer and settler at Jamestown.

sneak *v.* To creep secretly.

snip *n.* A single cut.

sol·emn (sol'ėm) *adj.* Serious; grave.

space cap'sṳle *n.* In a space vehicle, the small, sealed cabin that protects people or animals going into space.

Spain *n.* The country in southwestern Europe from which Christopher Columbus sailed.

Span'ïȧrd *n.* A person of the country of Spain.

Span'ish *n.* 1. The people of the country of Spain. 2. The language of Spain and many countries in Latin America. —*adj.* Of or belonging to the country of Spain.

spin'dle *n.* A rounded rod used to twist fibers into thread or to wind thread onto a spool.

Squän'tō *n.* The American Indian who taught the colonists of Plymouth the Indian methods of planting corn.

squäsh *n.* The fruit from a type of gourd plant.

squeal *n.* A loud, shrill cry.

squeal'ing *n.* The making of a loud, shrill cry.

stam·pēde' *n.* A sudden flight caused by fear.

State Dė·pärt'mėnt *n.* The department of the United States government that deals with the governments of other countries.

stat·ue (stach'ṳ) *n.* A figure of a person or animal.

stream *n.* A small, narrow river; a creek.

street'cär *n.* A vehicle that provides public transportation on a regular route and schedule and that usually runs on tracks; a trolley.

stub'ble *n.* Grain stalks left after the crop has been cut.

suf'frȧġe *n.* The right to vote.

Su·preme' Cōurt *n.* 1. In the United States, the highest court in the country, consisting of nine judges. 2. The building in which the Supreme Court meets.

swōōp *v.* To sweep down upon and seize.

tan *v.* To thrash; to spank.

tanned *adj.* Made into leather.

tär'dy *adj.* Slow; late; delayed.

tax *n.* Money given by a citizen to the government for the payment of the nation's expenses.

tē'pee *n.* An American Indian tent; a wigwam.

tĕr'rï·er *n.* Any of several types of small, active dogs formerly raised for hunting.

tĕr'ri·tō·ry *n.* A large area of land.

test pī'lŏt *n.* A person who flies a newly built aircraft to discover its strengths and weaknesses.

Tex'ås *n.* The twenty-eighth state admitted to the United States; the second largest state, located in the south-central United States.

Thañks·giv'ing *n.* In the United States, a national holiday for giving thanks to God, celebrated on the fourth Thursday of November.

thistle (this'le) *n.* A thorny plant with purple flowers.

thrĕad *n.* Fibers spun from cotton, linen, silk, or any other material.

thun'der·storm *n.* A brief storm of lightning and thunder, usually with rain and gusty winds.

tiñk'er *n.* A person who mends pots and pans.

'tis A contraction of *it is*.

tȯ·bac'cō *n.* The dried leaves of the tobacco plant prepared for smoking or chewing.

tod'dle *v.* To walk in short, uncertain steps, like a baby.

tȯ·mā'tō *or* **tȯ·mä'tō** *n.* A pulpy, red fruit that can be eaten.

tor'rĕnt *n.* A swiftly rushing stream.

tō'tĕm pole *n.* A pole with images of animals or natural objects carved and painted on it, erected by the Indians on the northwestern coast of North America.

trĕas'ȯre *n.* A store of valuables; any thing or person that is highly prized.

trī'añ·gle *n.* A figure with three sides and three angles.

Troy *n.* A city in eastern New York.

un·bė·liēv'ȧ·ble *n.* An event that is impossible to imagine happening.

un·con'scïȯus *adj.* Senseless; without physical or mental awareness.

un'der·ground *adj.* Secret; not open.

un·ėx·pect'ėd *adj.* Not foreseen; surprising.

un·ėx·plored' *adj.* Not searched; not mapped.

unsettled (un·set'tėld) *adj.* Uninhabited.

un·will'ing *adj.* Not ready; not eager.

up·set' *v.* To cause discomfort.

ush'er *n.* A person who takes people to their seats.

van'ish *v.* To pass from sight; to disappear.

ven'i·sȯn *n.* Deer meat prepared for eating.

vol·un·teer' *n.* One who serves because of a desire to do so, not because one has to.

voy'ȧġe *n.* A long trip by water; a journey by sea.

wāist   *n.* The narrow part of the body between the hips and the ribs.

war′rï·òr   *n.* A fighter.

Wäsh′ing·tòn, Geōrġe   *n.* The first president of the United States; commander of the American army during the Revolutionary War.

Wäsh′ing·tòn Mon′ū·mènt   *n.* A very tall, pointed building in Washington, D.C., honoring George Washington.

web·bing   *n.* Leather strips connecting the sections for the thumb and forefinger in a baseball glove or mitt.

wee   *adj.* Very small; tiny.

West, Ben′jà·min   *n.* A self-taught American painter who became president of the Royal Academy, a society founded by King George III to maintain the arts in England.

whirr   *n.* A humming sound.

White House   *n.* The official residence of the president of the United States, in Washington, D.C.

wig′wäm   *n.* An American Indian tent; a tepee.

wil′der·nèss   *n.* An unexplored land; a land not lived on by civilized people.

won′der·mènt   *n.* Amazement; awe.

woünd   *n.* A hurt; an injury.

wreck′àġe   *n.* The remains of something ruined or destroyed.

wring   *v.* To clasp and turn the hands.

yon′der   *adj.* Being over there; being in that direction.

200